GREAT HOUSES
OF
AMERICAN HISTORY

GREAT HOUSES
OF
AMERICAN HISTORY

by ANDREW H. HEPBURN

BRAMHALL HOUSE · NEW YORK

CONTENTS

GREAT HOUSES
OF
AMERICAN HISTORY

INTRODUCTION

Some dwellings are significant facets in the mosaic of history, and help tell the story of the settlement and development of a country. Though this story is told in terms of houses, it is also a chronicle of the domestic lives of many who helped establish and extend our nation.

The four-century progression of homes includes ancient desert dwellings that were there when the first settlers arrived in North America. It includes houses built by Spanish, English and Dutch settlers in the East and West. There are homes of patriots and colonial leaders who helped create the new nation. Some houses are special landmarks along the westward marching frontier. In a few lived political and military leaders of the War Between the States.

A special chapter describes some fascinating dwellings where renowned artists, writers and inventors lived and worked. Some houses, built in our nation's first era of affluence, are ornate monuments to great fortunes. In the same period other houses were homes of those who shaped this nation's destiny through leadership in government.

Space here permits inclusion of only a limited selection of important homes of history. Those chosen relate closely to the sweep of history through a succession of eight chapters, each devoted to an epoch of history. All the dwellings pictured and described in this pattern of national growth can be visited. Some are national monuments, many are national historic sites. Several are state monuments.

With intimate detail the famous homes reveal the lives of the people for whom they are remembered. In a special way this story of houses is also a chronicle of domestic architecture: ancient pueblo houses; primitive frontier cabins; colonial estate mansions and Dutch manor houses; simple Victorian dwellings and huge rambling Victorian homes; and in our own day the splendid mansions of millionaires.

Among those described are the birthplaces and homes of twelve Presidents of the United States; ancestral estates of three eminent American families; homes of two renowned soldiers. Two were palaces and seats of government. In one a war ended. In another a murdered President of the United States died. And in one a great Negro leader was born a slave.

I

PREHISTORIC DWELLINGS

The earliest exploration by Europeans of any area of what is now the United States began in 1540. That year Francisco Vasquez de Coronado led an expedition into the sunny Southwest, the region that is now Arizona, New Mexico and southern Colorado. Trekking north from Mexico the expedition roamed widely over the Southwest lured by reports of the fabled seven golden cities of Cíbola. Coronado did not find the cities, but he did find extensive and remarkable Indian communities that had been there a long time.

The Indian communities included substantial dwellings adapted to the dry heat of the Southwest, built of materials and by methods that the Spanish had never seen before. There were massive stone dwellings built within the caves of the cliffs, other houses—some on mesa tops—rising in tiers of several stories, were built with sun-dried slabs that came to be known as adobe.

The Indians living in the unusual dwellings that Coronado's men discovered were civilized and skillful. They cultivated a variety of foods, developed systems of irrigation, made pottery, wove baskets and cloth, and had elaborate tribal rituals. The homes they built are scattered all over the southwest region: in the high mountains, within the cliffs of canyons, and in bleak desert areas. Some are now in ruins, but others are still lived in—the oldest dwellings in continual use within the United States.

The origins of these prehistoric houses are lost in antiquity, but some are believed to have been built as early as the dawn of the Christian era. Several, are now preserved as historic monuments. A few of the most important of these abodes are described in the following pages. They include the large and spectacular cliff dwellings, two famous Pueblo communities (both still lived in), and a mysterious desert apartment house several stories high.

Cliff Dwellings of Mesa Verde, Colorado

Southern Colorado is high country, lofty tableland or mesas cut by deep rock-walled canyons. In some canyons sidewalls have eroded to make great caverns. In much of the area, canyon walls and mesa crests are heavily forested with superb stands of mountain trees: fir, ponderosa, pine, pinyon, juniper. It is dramatically beautiful country. One particularly handsome section, a forested mesa like a great fortress towering above surrounding valleys, with the mesa crest rising to more than eighty-five hundred feet, was named by Spanish traders who passed through the region more than two hundred years ago. They called it Mesa Verde, or "the green tableland."

But the Spanish traders did not explore the splendid forested mountain they named. Had they done so they might have discovered that the mesa crest and the caves in the canyon walls had been home sites for Indians who lived in the region for more than thirteen hundred years. Slowly, over the centuries, they developed an extraordinary and sophisticated culture including masonry cliff dwellings, the most remarkable prehistoric abodes in North America.

Notwithstanding the fact that the old Spanish trail linking Santa Fe with California passed close to Mesa Verde after 1776, almost nothing was known of the cliff dwellings or other ancient ruins of Mesa Verde until after 1850. Then various investigations began to reveal the story of Mesa Verde and the Indians who once lived on its crest and within the caves of its canyons. In 1859 a geological expedition reported on the character of Mesa Verde, but made no mention of the cliff dwellings. In 1874 W. H. Jackson, the pioneer photographer of the West, photographed some of the cliff houses from a distance. Finally in 1888 two ranchers who had lost cattle on the mesa top climbed down into the canyons of Mesa Verde in search of their cows. It is not reported whether the cows were found, but the ranchers did find, and reported with excitement, the existence of many cliff dwellings—whole communities of stone houses tucked into caves under the cliffs.

Very soon scientific expeditions began to unravel the story of the Mesa Verde people. Gradually a pattern of their life and development has emerged. In order to preserve the ruins and permit continued investigation and excavation Mesa Verde was made a fifty-one-thousand-acre national park in 1906. One of the most beautiful national parks, it is also one of the most fascinating to visit. Ruins, and the artifacts and relics found there, tell a story that goes back about two thousand years.

It is the story of the Pueblo Indians, thousands of whose descendants still live in the region, many in pueblos already built and occupied in 1540 when Coronado first roamed the land.

For purposes of clarity the story of the Pueblos is divided into four periods starting with a primitive era about the year 1 A.D. and ending about 1300 at Mesa Verde with the splendid, many-faceted highly advanced life of the cliff dwellers.

From deep inside a sandstone cave at Mesa Verde National Park, a camera catches the sunlit façade of the Cliff Palace, largest of all known cliff dwellings. *Photograph: Courtesy National Park Service.*

The first Pueblo Indians of the Mesa Verde region were farmers, as were all their descendants. They had no pottery but were expert weavers, making baskets calked with mud that held water and were used as primitive cooking vessels. They lived in pit houses on the mesa top, and probably in the caves of the mesa slopes. Their chief weapon—perhaps their only one —was the *atlatl,* a sharp-pointed throwing stick, deadly enough to kill game that provided hides for bags, robes and fur blankets. From stone, bone, wood and shells they made tools and implements, and fashioned jewelry. They raised corn and squash in small fields on the mesa top.

By about 400 A.D. the basket makers had made progress. They had learned to make pottery, and had either invented the bow and arrow or borrowed it from some other tribe. Substantial houses were built in caves and on the mesa top. Clustered in small villages, these were the first true pueblos. The Indians domesticated turkeys and used their feathers in many ways, and added the high protein bean to their diet. They developed better tools and began to import things like salt, turquoise and obsidian from other tribes.

Then about 700 A.D., the archaeologists say, began the first *true* Pueblo period, lasting about four hundred years and leading into the great or classic Pueblo epoch, the shining climax of Pueblo culture at Mesa Verde.

During this period the Indians of the region began to experiment with various building materials. They used posts and poles, stone and adobe in various combinations. They began to lay stone in courses, and to build dwellings with many rooms and of several stories. From somewhere outside the region they acquired cotton and wove it with great skill. They developed many types of pottery vessels, fired and decorated them. By about 1100 A.D. the Pueblo people of Mesa Verde were ready for the Pueblo golden age, the era of the great cliff dwellings.

Archaelogists think that this great Pueblo period at Mesa Verde lasted about two hundred years, ending with the gradual but complete abandonment of the cliff dwellings and the general area of Mesa Verde. Still unanswered is why the Pueblo people decided to move to the cliff caves in the first place, and why they subsequently left. It is possible that the move to the cliff caves may have been prompted by two factors: the growing threats from hostile tribes against the fortified pueblos on the mesa top, and easier access to water (the special topography of the region resulted in the emergence of springs near the base of the cliffs, closer to the cliff caves).

In any case, before the end of the period the Pueblo people had developed the most remarkable and astonishing community culture in the whole southwest region. The dwellings themselves and religious accessories associated with them are marvels of ingenuity and adaption, built with great skill and a knowledge of design and construction unequaled among other primitive people.

The edge of the Cliff Palace, Mesa Verde National Park— a jumble of stone walls and towers that was a community of several hundred people nearly one thousand years ago. *Photograph: Courtesy National Park Service.*

From across a canyon at Mesa Verde National Park, one can look down into the ruins of the largest known cliff dwelling and clearly see the intricate pattern of stone-walled towers and rooms which once housed a community of Pueblo Indians. *Photograph: Courtesy National Park Service.*

The ruins range from tiny storage rooms tucked away in almost inaccessible cliff niches to large villages containing scores of rooms, as many as two hundred in a single complex. Many of the ruins can easily be seen from overlooks along the canyon edge along the mesa top, linked by a road that provides access not only to the cliff dwellings, but to dozens of mesa top ruins, including remnants of the earliest dwellings, the primitive pit houses, some nearly two thousand years old.

Most visitors tend to concentrate on viewing and visiting the cliff dwellings. Some are within a short walk of Park Headquarters and its superb museum which preserves and explains a vast number of things relating to the life of the cliff dwellers.

Among the cliff dwellings and associated buildings of notable interest are the Spruce Tree House, the Sun Temple, a great ceremonial structure of the golden age, and the Cliff Palace, largest and most famous of the cliff dwellings and the first major ruin to be discovered. Also of interest are the Square Tower House, Sunset House, Mummy House, Oak Tree House, Fire Temple, an unusual ceremonial building in a cave, House of Many Windows and Balcony House.

Archaeologists say the cliff dwellers were well advanced and highly sophisticated, citing the vast number of artifacts and materials found in the caves that were part of the daily life at Mesa Verde. They include beautifully made and elaborately decorated pottery; samples of fabrics that show the cliff dwellers to have been master weavers; beautifully crafted examples of woodwork; weapons and utensils of all kinds; skillfully crafted and decorated jewelry. It is known that the walls of the cliff dwellings were plastered and decorated with designs in many colors.

The final Pueblo puzzle, still not fully explained, is the exodus of the Pueblo people from the region and the abandonment of the cliff dwellings in about 1300 A.D. Several reasons have been suggested: harassment by enemy tribes, soil that had lost its productivity; and, perhaps, more compelling than any other reason, drought. It is known that throughout the last quarter of the thirteenth century, from about 1275, a very severe drought occurred throughout the region. It must have made life at Mesa Verde almost impossible.

Where did the Pueblo people go? Probably to regions where flowing streams and their tributaries, such as the Rio Grande and the Little Colorado to the south and west, made water plentiful.

Perhaps, though there is no proof of it, the migrating Pueblo people from Mesa Verde helped settle the mesa tops and high mountains where Pueblo Indians still live in the sky city of Acoma and the great pueblo in the lofty beautiful mountains near Taos, New Mexico. Perhaps they even went as far west as the Gila River of Arizona, where, in about 1300, Pueblo people, accustomed to building many-storied houses, helped supplant a more ancient tribe of canal builders and built there a remarkable dwelling of packed earth called Casa Grande.

Acoma—The Sky City, *New Mexico*

In 1540 Hernando de Alvarado, a Spanish captain on a scouting mission from the main body of the Coronado expedition, sighted something remarkable among the bleak plains of what is now New Mexico. It appeared to be a large community of pueblos built on top of an apparently inaccessible flat-topped mountain, or mesa. Captain Alvarado reported his find to his chief Coronado, who mentioned it in the log of his expedition.

It was the first known report by a European of what is now the oldest continuously occupied community of houses in the United States. The Indians called it Akomi, meaning "people of the white rock." Captain Alvarado, misunderstanding his Indian scouts, called it Acuco. Today it is called Acoma, the Sky City. No one really knows how long the massive rock of Acoma has been the site of a community, but archaeologists believe that Indians lived on the rock and had built a pueblo there as early as 900 A.D. and that occupation has been continuous since 1075.

After Coronado other Spanish explorers reported seeing Acoma. In 1563 Antonio de Espejo described a steep trail cut in the side of the cliff leading to the top, thus explaining how the Indians managed to carry timbers and other material to the crest of the mesa. But it was 1598 before Spanish soldiers gained the crest of the rock and saw the ancient and extensive community there. In that same year citizens of the pueblo submitted to the authority of the Spanish crown as represented by Don Juan de Onate. It was a grudging, hostile submission. The Acoma Indians opposed the authority of Spain with bloody incidents of revolt. A lull in the hostilities came in 1629 with the arrival of a missionary priest, Fray Juan Ramirez. Unarmed and alone he won the loyalty and admiration of the dwellers on the rock by seemingly miraculous feats of heroism and healing. After that Acoma dwellers became followers of the redoubtable Father Ramirez, and under his direction built an amazing church, unique in North America.

It was not until 1863 that the Acoma Indians won undisputed possession of their mesa and the valley grazing lands around it. Their rights were confirmed by a most unusual treaty following a visit to Washington by the chiefs of the tribe and a meeting there with President Lincoln.

Acoma today, within a few miles of a super highway, Interstate 40, that sweeps across the desert to the north, probably looks about as it did when first seen by Spanish soldiers in 1540, except for its church. Acoma rises abruptly from the dry windswept plains that surround it. The fairly level

▷
Acoma Pueblo, ancient,
still-lived-in community of
Pueblo Indians, which stands
on a four-hundred-foot mesa.
*Photograph: Courtesy New
Mexico State Tourist Bureau.*

flat-top covering of about seventy acres is nearly four hundred feet above the surrounding plain, and its deeply eroded walls are almost sheer. From a distance the pueblo appears to be part of the rock itself. Dwellings of stone and adobe one thousand feet long and forty feet high extend in three parallel lines running east and west along the crest. Each of the three dwellings consists of three stories terraced in the usual pueblo style. Originally the first story, rising from twelve to fifteen feet and used entirely for storage, had no openings except for trapdoors on top. Ladders that could be pulled up linked the ground floor with the second floor. But the third story and roof could only be reached by steep, narrow steps against the division walls. Though the long rows of houses suggest a communal life, the dwelling place of each family is private, separated from others by solid walls. The house groups flank streets. One street wider than the others provides a plaza for ceremonies and festivals. Rising higher than the flat-topped dwelling groups, dominating the whole crest of the rock, is the remarkable church, built under the direction of Father Ramirez after his arrival at Acoma in 1629. Called San Esteban Rey Mission, it was named for the patron saint of the Acoma people, St. Stephen, whose day, September 2, is celebrated by a big, colorful festival that draws members of the Acoma tribe from miles away.

14

Today most visitors arrive by an unpaved highway, New Mexico 23, leading south from Interstate 40 (US 66) about fifteen miles west of Albuquerque. As they near Acoma Rock tourists see to the north Enchanted Mesa, rising about one hundred feet higher than Acoma Rock. Legends of the Acoma tribe say that it was once their tribal home, but that a violent storm closed the only trail to the top, leaving members of the tribe trapped there to die of starvation.

Upon reaching Acoma Rock visitors have a choice of several trails to the summit. If rugged enough they can climb by the historic ladder trail, an ancient toe and finger hole trail on the north side, believed to be the only trail leading to the summit before 1629. Still called Camino del Padre, it was the trail used by Father Ramirez to make his renowned ascent. The good father later provided what is now known as the Burro Trail, a less hazardous route, and the one over which were carried all the timbers and materials used in building the church. Most visitors now use a more modern foot trail, a combination of steep path and steps, not difficult for most people.

At the crest visitors can see typical Acoma homes, some of the oldest still lighted by windows of selenite, mined nearby. Each dwelling has primitive facilities for grinding corn, unchanged in hundreds of years. Once a year, before the festival of St. Stephen, inside walls of the houses are freshly whitewashed, and garments of skins and blankets, guns, trinkets of all kinds, and silver jewelry made by Acoma artisans are hung on them. There are twisted strings of red chili peppers, bags of dried fruit, and meat hung from the beams. At night wool *colchones* (mattresses) are laid on the floor; during the day they are rolled to make comfortable seats. All cooking done in Acoma homes is done outside in beehive-shaped ovens.

Acoma pottery, thin-walled and somewhat fragile, gaily decorated with flowers, birds and trees, as well as a limited offering of primitive silver jewelry made by Acoma craftsmen, and also gay blankets are for sale.

Though visitors may find many houses in the Acoma community fascinating, they are likely to be overwhelmed by the aspect and character of the San Esteban Mission, one of the finest and largest of all pueblo missions and a marvel of adobe construction. Almost starkly simple in design, the front walls, windowless except for a square opening over the entrance, are sloped to form massive buttresses, topped by square towers and open belfries. The church proper is one hundred fifty feet long and forty feet wide, with walls ten feet thick rising sixty feet.

Though the church is remarkable, even more remarkable is the fact that it could be built at all. Every ounce of earth and rock used was carried up the steep trail to the top of the mesa in baskets on the backs of devout Indian women. The heavy roof beams, each forty feet long by fourteen inches square, were cut in the Cebollata Mountains, thirty miles away, and carried on the backs of men, along with other timbers used in the building. The austerity of the exterior of the church contrasts sharply with the interior, where more than two hundred years of devotion, ingenuity and craftsmanship have provided a nave set with richly carved and painted reredos

divided into panels, as well as other ornate symbols and souvenirs of faith. Most precious of all the displays of the church is a painting of the Acoman patron saint, St. Stephen, believed to have been given to Father Ramirez by King Charles II of Spain and said to possess miraculous powers. The Acoma people believe that as long as they possess the painting they will be prosperous, their crops bountiful. Once a neighboring pueblo, Laguna, suffering from drought and epidemics, borrowed the miraculous canvas and almost at once their afflictions ended. It took a lawsuit to get it back to Acoma.

Usually displayed in the church the painting is a unique symbol of political authority, confirming the tribe's control of their lands, originally granted by Spain in 1659. A treaty with the United States of 1858 confirmed their ownership of the land but the Acoma and other tribes concerned with the treaty delayed final settlement of the boundaries until 1863. Then seven tribal governors went to Washington to confer with President Lincoln, who gave each governor a silver-headed cane engraved "A. Lincoln Prst. U.S.A. [name of the tribe] 1863." The Acoma cane, displayed in the church, is the official badge of office for each succeeding governor. The treaty also included Acoma Rock, and extensive valley acres where crops were grown and herds were grazed. Now the tribal lands spread over 113,000 arid acres, most of it fit only for grazing.

Adjoining the church is the consecrated burying ground of the mission, perhaps the only one of its kind in the world. Because there is no soil on the crest of Acoma Rock, and because Acoma converts wanted their dead buried in consecrated ground, they built a stone retaining wall ten feet high enclosing an area two hundred feet square, then filled the area with thousands of sacksfuls of earth carried from the plain below.

Taos Pueblo, New Mexico

For Captain Hernando de Alvarado 1540 was an important year. As leader of a band of Spanish soldiers who had trekked north from Mexico with the expedition headed by Captain General Francisco Coronado, he had been dispatched to the northeast. Captain Alvarado was no more successful than Coronado in discovering the golden cities. But he did discover two remarkable communities and thereby achieved a measure of fame.

The first, of course, was Acoma. Later, while climbing among the high forested slopes, which the Spanish named Sangre de Cristo Mountains, he discovered and explored an Indian community living in two extraordinary five-storied buildings, combined apartments, and a fortress. The community came to be called Taos Pueblo, or San Geronimò de Taos.

Taos Pueblo is still a busy Indian community, home of about fifteen hundred Pueblo Indians, direct descendants of Indians who occupied it when Captain Alvarado paid his visit in 1540, and probably little changed in aspect or character from that time. Archaeologists agree that Taos is the oldest and perhaps the largest continually occupied apartment dwelling in

Dwellers in Acoma, the Sky City, found water for their needs at the base of a four-hundred-foot cliff reached by precipitous trails.
Photograph: Courtesy New Mexico State Tourist Bureau.

17

About fifteen hundred Pueblo Indians live in Taos Pueblo, the largest in the Southwest, seen here from across the mountain river Pueblo de Taos, spanned by a log bridge. *Photograph: Courtesy New Mexico Department of Development.*

the United States, probably in the world. They believe that it was probably built at least eight hundred years ago by Indians migrating from more arid regions to the north and west, seeking reliable sources of water. They found abundant water in the Rio Pueblo de Taos that tumbles down the slopes of Taos Mountain rising to more than eight thousand feet behind the pueblo. They diverted the water for irrigation, and still do.

The story of Taos, largest and most famous of some twenty still occupied pueblos along the Rio Grande River valley in New Mexico, is quickly told. There is no mystery about it, as there is about the much older, remarkable cliff dwellings of Mesa Verde to the north and west, whose ruins intrigue and puzzle archaeologists. Some think that the Pueblo Indians who built Taos may have migrated from Mesa Verde, when water became scarce there.

At Mesa Verde the life of the communities tucked into the cliffs is a matter of conjecture whereas there is none about the Taos Pueblo. Any one who visits the pueblo today can see what it is, and what it probably has been for hundreds of years: two large communal buildings of adobe brick, plastered with mud dried to a mellow tan. The buildings face each other separated by the Rio Taos flowing across a large central plaza, bridged by huge hand-hewn pine logs. Until about 1890 the only entrance to the terraced rooms was by means of ladders that were drawn up when the community was threatened. In recent years, windows and doors have been cut into the walls, probably the only change in the buildings since 1540. But ladders still remain on the outside since the big dwellings contain no inside stairways between floors.

The two large main buildings are surrounded by smaller houses. Much of the life and activity of the community is outdoors. There, wooden platforms are used to protect stored corn, alfalfa and other crops grown in irrigated fields near the pueblo. Their method of irrigation is probably the oldest continually used system in the country. Cone-shaped *hornos,* or ovens, where all communal baking is done, are scattered among the buildings. Here and there are underground *kivas,* or council chambers, reached by ladders protruding from the ground. In the *kivas* men of the tribe hold their meetings and teach boys their ancient ceremonies and traditions. Visitors are not allowed in the *kivas,* and women of the tribe are admitted only on ceremonial occasions.

The interiors of the pueblo buildings, where each family has one or more rooms, can be seen by special arrangement. Blankets and skins are on the floors and walls, dried peppers and other dried foods hang from ceiling rafters along with strings of gay beads. Colorful traditional ceremonial garments and feathered ornaments used in ceremonial dances hang from pegs in the walls.

Though the Taos tribe are strict traditionalists, doing most things as their ancestors have done them, they make some concessions to modern ways in their associations with their neighbors in the Taos area. Most Taos Indians are farmers and stockmen and have no objection to using reasonably modern farm tools. Both men and women work as servants in Taos households, or as gardeners, garage helpers, truck and car drivers. Some of the men maintain full ceremonial regalia, which they don on notice to pose for photographers and artists, for varying fees. Generally speaking, the members of the Taos tribe are well adjusted to modern life, and are in no way hostile.

But they were not always so peaceful. Following the year 1540, almost from the first appearance of Spanish priests and soldiers, Taos Indians were openly hostile, sometimes violently so. Spanish settlers first came to the area about 1615, and in 1617 built a church under the direction of Father Pedro Mirana. Later, during the insurrection of the Pueblo Indians led by the Taos Pueblos throughout the whole area, the church was burned. Taos Indians led an anti-American revolt in 1847, and destroyed another church, whose massive ruins still stand at the entrance to the pueblo.

Of all the still occupied pueblos of the southwest Taos is the easiest and most rewarding to visit. Taos Indians welcome visitors, permit them to take photographs, peer within the pueblo buildings, and watch the spectacular ceremonial dances, which are part of the way of life for Taos Indians. Sightseeing fees add substantial sums to community coffers as do the sales of typical Taos Indian craft products, such as mocassins, drums and pottery. Another standard fee-producing activity is posing in ceremonial regalia for artists and photographers.

Taos Pueblo is open to visitors sunup to sundown, and is easily found about two and a half miles north of Taos village, on New Mexico Highway 3 (off US 64), about seventy miles northeast of New Mexico's capital city, Santa Fe.

Casa Grande, Arizona

The fame of Father Eusebio Francisco Kino, Jesuit priest and missionary explorer of the American Southwest, rests chiefly on his establishment of several missions in the desert region of what is now southern Arizona. They include Tumacacori near Tubac and San Xavier del Bac near the present city of Tucson. But Father Kino also earned fame as an archaeologist by discovering and naming what is generally regarded as the most unusual prehistoric structure in southern Arizona, the Casa Grande in the Gila River Valley, southeast of present-day Phoenix.

The discovery occurred in 1694 when Father Kino and his followers were trudging north from Sonora, Mexico, across the desert plain. Nearing the Gila River he sighted something strange towering above the sand and sagebrush. Coming closer he saw that it was a square building of dried earth rising about the equivalent of four stories, within the center of a compound of many abandoned and crumbling lesser buildings, all within a thick earthen wall enclosing about two acres. The area all around was laced with trenches and ditches, which Father Kino rightly assumed must have been part of an extensive system of irrigation. He noted that some of the larger canals, as much as twenty-five feet wide and fifteen feet deep, were so well preserved that they could still be used for irrigation.

In the desert of southern Arizona near the ruins of Casa Grande is a mysterious and very old multi-storied building, now protected by a metal umbrella. *Photograph: Courtesy Tucson News Service.*

20

Father Kino named the towering building that dominated the abandoned community, Casa Grande, or "the big house." Now preserved as a national monument it still bears that name. Of it Father Kino wrote: "The Casa Grande is a four-story building as large as a castle and equal to the finest church in Sonora." A more specific and detailed description was made in 1697 by Lieutenant Juan Mange, who returned to Casa Grande with Father Kino on a later expedition. He wrote that the central building had walls so smooth that they resembled planed boards and that much of the lower courses of masonry was polished like pueblo pottery. At that time the whole community was in an excellent state of preservation, but less than a hundred years later travelers through the region reported that the central tower, all the buildings around it and the surrounding wall and canals were in an advanced state of deterioration. It would be another hundred years before any serious attempt was made to solve the mystery of the Casa

Grande community and its remarkable tower, which has been called America's first skyscraper. Starting with a Smithsonian expedition in 1891 and followed by a succession of other archaeological expeditions, the riddle of the prehistoric occupation of the desert valley of the Gila River has been substantially solved.

Archaeologists believe that farming began in the Gila Valley as early as the beginning of the Christian era. Primitive villages of single room huts made of brush and mud were built and shallow irrigation ditches dug. Crops raised were maize (corn), beans, pumpkins and cotton. Gradually, over a period of several hundred years, the irrigation system was extended, the canals made wider, longer, and deeper. Irrigated fields spread over the valley, the first known system of irrigation in what is now the United States. It is believed that the knowledge of farming methods may have come from the south, from the Indians of Mexico. But the origin of the Gila River Valley farmers, or canal diggers, is still not known. Pima Indians, who came to the area later and are still there, called the canal diggers the Hohokam, or the "ancient ones." Over a period of several hundred years the civilization of the Hohokam people became more complex and sophisticated. They built bigger and better houses. They cremated their dead. They greatly extended and improved their system of irrigation. They had high skills in crafts, carving shells (which must have come from the Gulf of California two hundred miles to the west) and stone, making necklaces, rings and bracelets, some intricately inlaid with turquoise. They developed mosaics and learned how to weave fine cloth.

But the Hohokam people did not build Casa Grande, or the extensive compound of buildings and walls that surround it. It is believed that in about 1000 A.D. tribes of Pueblo Indians began to drift into the arid valley of the Gila River from mountain regions to the north. The Pueblo people knew how to build thick-walled many-roomed dwellings of stone and packed earth or adobe, having built them in mountain caves and on top of mesas to the north and east. They began to build them in the flat plain of the Gila River valley, in and among and finally replacing the dwellings of the Hohokam people.

The Casa Grande was a pueblo building. It served a dual purpose, as a dwelling, with many rooms (eleven large ones), that probably accommodated several families, and as a watch tower from which unwelcome visitors coming across the open plain could be seen for many miles. As a further protection the Casa Grande builders erected thick, high walls around each of several compounds.

It is believed that Casa Grande and the associated walls and buildings that make up several villages were completed sometime around 1300 A.D., and were used and occupied for perhaps two hundred years. Exactly why they were finally abandoned is not known, but it is thought that several centuries of irrigation without fertilizing had waterlogged the fields so that they no longer produced adequate crops. In any case, the descendants of the Casa Grande builders began to drift away in search of better farmland.

Thus the community had been abandoned almost two hundred years when Father Kino discovered it. That its preservation was as good as he described it then is considered remarkable.

The ruins of Casa Grande and the remnants of eight villages and sections of ancient canals are preserved today within 472 acres. Visitors will find the ruins about two miles north of the town of Coolidge (fifty-six miles southeast of Phoenix), on Arizona Highway 87, a few miles east of Interstate 10 connecting Phoenix with Tucson.

The story of Casa Grande and its associated buildings is vividly told in a well-appointed Visitors Center. Only visitors with a high interest in archaeology will find anything worth inspecting outside of the Casa Grande itself, though all the surrounding villages have been or are being excavated, and have yielded a treasure of artifacts and relics. No attempt to restore Casa Grande has been made, though an extraordinary umbrella of steel has been built above it to check further erosion of its crumbling walls.

The building is unique. In the United States no other prehistoric relic even remotely approaches it in character. Equally unusual is the method of construction. The material used, in addition to timber, was caliche, a clay of high lime content found about four feet below the surface of the desert. When tamped wet into walls it dries to almost rocklike hardness. Neither adobe brick nor stone, both familiar building materials among the Pueblo Indians, were available. The Pueblo builders who wanted Casa Grande to be a high building were afraid that caliche simply packed into thick walls would not stand the strains. So they built one story in courses of packed earth twenty-five inches high to a height of seven feet, then filled the area within the walls with dirt, making an artificial hill seven feet high, with the rest of Casa Grande built three stories higher above the earth-filled foundation.

The massive walls of the eleven rooms of the building had no windows, only large round holes cut here and there, believed to provide light and ventilation. However, several openings called calendar holes were drilled through the walls at such angles and positions that the sun shone through them only on certain days of the year. The ancient Egyptians and the Indians of Mexican Yucatan did the same thing in their temples. But Casa Grande was not a temple or religious building. It was an apartment house and watchtower combined.

When first explored, the living quarters of Casa Grande were strewn with many of the accessories of day-to-day living: cooking and storage pottery, sleeping mats, corncobs and bits of cloth. These suggested that the former inhabitants had left suddenly. Most of the relics of occupation were broken or pilfered by a succession of curious visitors, but many have been salvaged and can be seen in the Visitors Center or in various museums of the Southwest.

24

II

SPANISH SETTLERS

Settlements of Imperial Spain in the area that is now the United States occurred in three widely separated regions: Florida, New Mexico and coastal California.

Florida's settlement grew from a defensive posture to prevent French colonists from encroaching on tropical Florida that Ponce de Leon had discovered in 1513 and claimed for Spain. In 1565 Spain established a bastion of empire in Florida at the place where Ponce de Leon landed. It became, in time, a village called St. Augustine, the oldest European community in the United States. One house survived fire and siege, and was modified and extended over three hundred years to become, the Historical Society of St. Augustine claims, the oldest continuously occupied house in this country.

Spanish efforts to settle New Mexico were quite different from those in Florida. In New Mexico settlements were carefully planned to accommodate a large-scale migration from Spanish Mexico. The administrative core was the superbly located community of Sante Fe, where, in 1609, the splendid and unique Palace of Governors was built as a dwelling and headquarters. It has housed a long line of governors from three nations for more than three hundred years.

Spain's claim to California rested on that region's discovery in 1542 by a Portuguese mariner in the service of Spain, Juan Rodrigues Cabrillo. But Spain did nothing about settling California for more than two hundred years. Then, disturbed by the knowledge that Russian fur traders were establishing fortified settlements along the coast of northern California, the ambitious Spanish governor of Mexico set about colonizing California. Planned with skill and carried out with dispatch, it involved several elements: presidios, or garrisons, at strategic points; pueblos, or civic centers for nonmilitary colonists; a chain of missions along the coast; and cattle

A curious melange of 300 years of change, this picturesque dwelling on a quiet St. Augustine street is believed to have been begun about 1600, and so may be the nation's oldest house. *Photograph: Courtesy Florida State Tourist Board.*

25

ranches based on grants of huge tracts of land. The presidios and pueblos grew from tiny settlements into the great cities of California: San Diego, Los Angeles and San Francisco. The twenty-one missions are now graceful relics of California's colorful past. But the great Spanish ranch houses have disappeared, with the exception of a huge adobe dwelling in northern California built by General Mariano Vallejo, last Spanish Mexican governor of California. Now one of California's most historic houses, it is preserved by the state as a memorial of the period of Spanish settlement.

Oldest House, St. Augustine, Florida

In 1513, 21 years after Columbus proclaimed his discovery of the New World, Ponce de Leon, a Spanish adventurer who had been with Columbus, sailed west from the islands of the Caribbean and came ashore on a tropical mainland coast. It was Easter Sunday so he named the new land "Florida" (the Feast of Flowers), and claimed it for the King of Spain. But Ponce de Leon, who sought gold and a legendary spring which conferred eternal youth on those who drank from it, left no mark on the new land.

Fifty-two years later in 1565, at the place where Ponce de Leon landed, a Spanish leader named Don Pedro Menendez, captain general of the Spanish treasure fleets, established a military camp, an outpost from which he hoped to destroy nearby settlements of French Huguenot colonists. He massacred the French, but his camp in the tropical wilderness remained, first a bastion of empire, growing slowly into a fortified village and then a town—St. Augustine, oldest town in the area of what is now the United States.

St. Augustine grew precariously and slowly. Twelve years after its establishment there were eighty soldiers along with their families, most of them from the Canary Islands. For living quarters they built primitive houses, little more than huts, of either plank and thatch or all thatch. Some of the larger ones had floors of tapia or tabby, a mixture of sand, lime and shell. All the houses were inflammable. And burn they did. The English, bitter enemies of Spain, saw to that. Sir Francis Drake sacked and burned the settlement in 1586. During the first thirty-five years Indians attacked several times, drove the settlers inside the wooden fort and burned their houses.

Drake left a written record of the character of the town and a rude map: ". . . a little town or village without walls, built of wooden houses, as the plot doth plainly show." The plot, first map of any community in the area of the United States, shows Drake's proud invasion fleet clustered around the mouth of the Anastasia River, with landing barges opposite a cluster of little houses on the west bank of the river south of a fort. An early Spanish map drawn a little later gives more detail: a dock extending into the river, a scattering of houses on the riverbank among patches of cultivated fields, which Drake had described as "delightful gardens."

One of the houses, probably built toward the end of the sixteenth century or very early in the seventeenth century, with a foundation solid enough

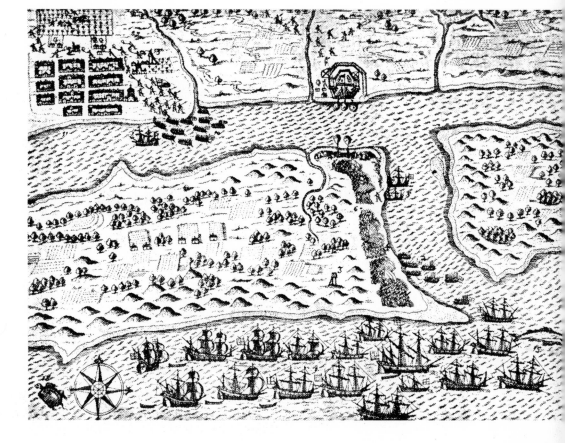

In 1586 the Elizabethan seadog Sir Francis Drake, discovering St. Augustine by accident, sacked and burned the little town. The map shows the town as he found it, with Drake's fleet offshore. The mapmaker describes it as "a little town without walls, built of wooden houses as the plot doth plainly show." *Courtesy Florida State Historical Society.*

to stand the ravages of fire and weather, served as a base for future building. It has given historians enough evidence of permanence to claim it is the oldest house built in the area of what is now the United States.

St. Augustine's house, a curious melange of additions and changes over a period of almost three hundred years, is now one of that remarkable city's most fascinating exhibits, drawing a stream of curious visitors. It is a composite of several architectural periods, starting with early Spanish and ending with recent Victorian; its story is richly interwoven with events of the city's past and the lives of many owners.

Exhaustive research has failed to reveal who built the first house on the site or the identity of those who lived in it during the first hundred or more years. Investigators believe that it probably began sometime after 1600 as a primitive hut, perhaps more substantial than its neighbors.

In any case, whatever house stood on the site before 1700 it was destroyed by fire in 1702, following the siege and capture of the village by Governor James Moore of South Carolina, the most destructive of many conflagrations that beset St. Augustine from earliest days.

Undoubtedly at least part of the present house was built soon after that. The first documented occupant was Thomas Gonzales Hernando, one of the Canary Islanders who migrated to St. Augustine during the early

Spanish days. Parish records show that he married Francisca de Guevarra in 1723. Cathedral records reveal that a child of that marriage was buried in the cathedral churchyard in 1727. The Gonzales family still lived in the house in 1763 when Spain ceded Florida to England, in exchange for Havana, Cuba, which had been recently captured by the British. By that time St. Augustine had grown considerably and had more than three thousand Spanish residents. Thomas Gonzales was more than sixty years old and in poor health. Unable to sell his house he deeded it to Juan Jose de la Puente, appointed by the Spanish authorities to make an inventory of all houses in the community. Puente, in turn, sold the house to an English trader, first of several English owners. One, Joseph Peavett, was the most prosperous. He claimed to own more than three thousand acres of land, fifty-seven slaves, four horses and some cattle. Another, an Irish soldier who acquired the house by marrying Peavett's widow, was so profligate that the house was soon put up for sale to satisfy his debts. At the sale in 1790, Geronimo Alvarez, a Spaniard, acquired the house for 942 pesos. Alvarez was a baker by trade and a politician; he was successful at both. The family became well-to-do, and Alvarez became mayor, and later, under President John Quincy Adams, Keeper of the Public Archives for east Florida. His family owned the house until 1882.

Soon after that the fame of the picturesque old house, and public interest in it, prompted an owner, Dr. C. P. Carver, a dentist, to show his house to visitors for a fee. Successive owners continued to exhibit it until its acquisition by the St. Augustine Historical Society in 1918. The Society made exhaustive investigations into the history of the house, undertook to restore it to its 1875 appearance, and refitted and furnished it with effects characteristic of all the periods of its use, starting with the earliest Spanish period.

As visitors move through the house today they glimpse in the structure, style and furnishings, the history of north Florida. The first floor, with thick walls of coquine stone from quarries on nearby Anastasia Island, is early Spanish. Its furnishings include Spanish pieces of the sixteenth and seventeenth centuries. Woodwork is done in the almost indestructible Florida red cedar. First floor rooms include a Spanish kitchen, opening into a walled and arcaded patio with a unique garden. In it grows plants and flowers native to Florida, along with migrants from other lands, all carefully labeled.

It is believed that the early Spanish house was one story, probably with a thatched roof. The timbered second floor, reached by narrow stairs, has English furnishings, early nineteenth century merging into Victorian. It also reflects the greater prosperity of more recent owners in a certain elegance of decor and appointments.

To prove its claims, the Historical Society of St. Augustine maintains an extensive museum in an adjoining building with exhibits of artifacts and relics demonstrating the house's slow evolution from a simple thatched hut to the multiroomed dwelling of a prosperous family.

Palace of Governors, Santa Fe, New Mexico

While Spain clung desperately to its tiny beachhead established on the east coast of North America, impressive plans were being made in the high councils of the Spanish government in Mexico City to control and develop Spanish claims to vast regions in western North America. The plans began to bear fruit early in the seventeenth century with the dispatch of soldiers and settlers to establish a capital for the province of New Mexico. It was to extend from the Mississippi to the Pacific and from Mexico as far north as people roamed. The expedition's leader was Don Pedro de Peralta, governor of the huge wilderness province. In the winter of 1609 he led troops and settlers north, crossed the Rio Grande and marched east into the forested foothills of the beautiful Sangre de Cristo Mountains. Spain had prior knowledge of the region, as it had been described many years before by one of Coronado's men who had climbed into the mountains and discovered the big Indian pueblo called Taos.

But Governor Peralta stopped short of Taos, choosing a site for the new capital in a little valley on the banks of the Rio de Santa Fe, with mountain slopes rising all around. It was a splendid choice—few community sites in the country can claim better locations. The Pueblo Indians who lived in the area called it Kuapoga, but Peralta gave it a much longer and more florid name—La Villa Real de la Santa Fe de San Francisco. Everyone knows it today as Santa Fe, New Mexico, the oldest seat of government in the United States, and one of the most unusual cities in North America.

With very un-Spanish energy Peralta began building a walled city or presidio, an all-purpose fortress including a *palacio* and a spacious plaza. The palace was to be the governor's home. Except for a few years when it was held by rebellious Indians, it remained the official residence of a long line of Spanish governors, governors representing the new nation of Mexico, and territorial governors of the United States.

Both historically and architecturally the Palace of Governors is one of the most remarkable and interesting houses in the country. The long, low building, still very much as it probably appeared when completed in 1610, though smaller than the original presidio, is no conventional palace. It extends about four hundred feet along the north side of Santa Fe's historic plaza. As first built in 1609 it extended north about eight hundred feet, with the whole area surrounded by an adobe wall. All buildings within this enclave were known in early Spanish times as Casa Reales, or Royal Houses. They included the palace proper, home and office for the governor, quarters for soldiers, and a few buildings used by the government. Two low towers stood at either end of the plaza side, one a storehouse for military supplies, the other a chapel for the garrison. A covered porch extended along the entire plaza side very much as it does today. During Spanish days it was a convenient place for hanging prisoners. Today it is the city's favorite marketplace for the exhibit and sale of wares made by Hopi and Pueblo Indians.

In structure and design the palace is almost pure Pueblo, the earliest known adaption of Spanish methods and ideas to indigenous material used by Indians from prehistoric times. The material is adobe brick, or brick of dried mud, with surfaces plastered. There are no arches. Roofs are flat, roof beams often extending out from the walls, supported by rough wooden posts, an idea borrowed directly from the Indians. Walls are very thick, windows and openings few. The building now is a hollow rectangle with a grassy patio at the center.

Few dwellings in the country have had a more vigorous and varied life. During early Spanish days the palace was the center for development of the region, and extension of the Catholic faith throughout the Southwest. The handful of Franciscan friars were kept busy. Eight years after the establishment of the colony they had built eleven churches and converted fourteen thousand Indians to the Roman Catholic faith.

But the padres' methods of conversion were not always gentle. Not infrequently Indians were flogged or even hanged for refusing to become Christians. Frequently small revolts occurred among the Indians, and occasionally rebellion flared on a large scale, particularly in the famed region-

The Palace of Governors, Santa Fe, New Mexico, built in 1610, served as an official residence of many governors for over 250 years. *Photograph: Courtesy New Mexico Department of Development.*

The long porch of the ancient Palace of Governors, which faces Santa Fe's historic plaza, is a favorite marketplace where Indian wares are exhibited and sold. *Photograph: Courtesy Fred Harvey.*

wide revolt of 1680, when three thousand Indians besieged the palace, finally seized it, and made it their headquarters for twelve years, converting the building into a pueblo and the chapel into a *kiva*. It took Spain twelve years to regain control and reestablish the palace as provincial headquarters.

After that, little happened to the palace itself. For over a period of 130 years it was the official residence of twenty-eight Spanish governors. Then, for twenty-five years the new nation of Mexico sent governors to live in the palace. After 1846 came the territorial governors of the United States who added Victorian furnishings and decoration to a collection of Spanish fittings and furniture. One territorial governor was General Lew Wallace. Visitors to the palace today can see his portrait in the room he used as a study, along with the chair where he sat while writing the novel *Ben Hur*.

The palace ceased to be a residence after 1907, when an executive mansion was built. In 1909, after renovation and careful restoration, the palace became the site of the Museum of New Mexico. Curiously, the best plans to guide restoration were found in the British Museum in London.

The museum re-creates the character of several of the palace rooms during the period of official residence; superb exhibits, relics, art, sculpture, artifacts and implements give visitors the best possible opportunity to understand the life and times during centuries of Spanish rule. Several rooms are devoted to prehistory, including the classic period of Pueblo development. There is an early Spanish colonial room, a late Spanish colonial room, a room devoted to the Mexican period, and finally the Territorial room, covering the period from 1846 to 1912, where, among other exhibits in addition to General Lew Wallace's portrait and chair, stands a piano that was once hauled across the plains on the Santa Fe Trail by oxcart. It can still make music.

The period rooms of the Palace of Governors exhibit costumes and furnishings typical of its more than 250 years as an official residence of governors. *Photograph: Courtesy New Mexico State Tourist Bureau.*

The historic palace is easy to find and visit. It extends along the north side of Santa Fe's handsome central plaza, on Palace Avenue, a few blocks east of US route 64 leading to Taos, north and east of Interstate 25 swinging along the southern edge of the city.

About three blocks south of the plaza the Santa Fe flows east to west, its course controlled by flood-walls. Just south of the river are two buildings that relate to the earliest Spanish period. They are the tiny San Miguel Church, oldest mission church in the country, built about 1635 for the use of converted Indian slaves of Spanish officials and, just north of the old church, across Canyon Road, an ancient house that is both a curiosity and a mystery. No one knows when it was built or by whom, but the citizens of Santa Fe insist that it stood beside the river when Governor Peralta established his provincial capital in 1609, and perhaps many years before that, so it is likely to be the oldest Spanish house in the United States. Santa Fe's oldest house is tiny, a square block of puddled adobe with ceiling beams extending through the walls in traditional Pueblo style. Though now a museum it attracts few visitors, notwithstanding a bold sign acclaiming it to be the nation's oldest house.

Residents of Santa Fe call this tiny adobe house in the heart of Sante Fe, New Mexico, the nation's oldest house. *Photograph: Courtesy New Mexico Department of Development.*

Vallejo Houses, California

On the frontier of California, Mariano Guadalupe Vallejo was an important man. Born in 1808 in Monterey County he grew up during the last years of Spanish control, which ended in 1822. Soon after Vallejo joined the Mexican Army, and rose quickly to the rank of general. Within a few years he undertook important missions for the new government in controlling settlement of the northern frontier, acquired 150,000 acres of land on which he established huge ranches, founded the Pueblo of Sonoma, and built two unusual homes, both now state historical monuments.

General Vallejo left his special mark on California in the region just north of San Francisco Bay, now a richly fertile land of low forested mountains patched with some of California's oldest and finest vineyards. Towns in the region today include Santa Rosa, famed for the gardens and home of the gentle plant wizard Luther Burbank; Petaluma, Napa, a vineyard center; and Sonoma, which General Vallejo founded.

But in Vallejo's day most of the north Bay region was a splendid wilderness, where tribes of hostile Indians lived. Russian settlers from Fort Ross on the coast to the west were beginning to filter in. The Indians resented settlement of any kind. The Russians were concerned with poaching fur seals and otter in offshore waters that belonged to Mexico. It was the dual threat of Indians and Russians that led to Vallejo's mission from the Mexican government. His orders were to colonize the wilderness frontier, pacify the Indians, and fend off the Russians. Young Vallejo set about his assignment with energy and enthusiasm. An early step taken about 1833 was the establishment of Rancho Petaluma, now often referred to as the Petaluma Adobe, on sixty-six thousand acres granted to him by the Mexican government.

Rancho Petaluma was developed on a grand scale. The ranchhouse was huge, the largest adobe dwelling in northern California. Three facades shaded by broad balconies extended more than two hundred feet each. The adobe walls were three feet thick, and the frame of the house was built from massive hand-hewn timbers cut from tall trees in the mountains to the north, and then dragged to the site by oxcarts. The great beams were bound in place by rawhide thongs. Not a nail was used. A fourth side of the rambling house was a spacious patio, center of ranch activity and a training headquarters where Indians learned to ride as *vaqueros*. At the ranchhouse the planting and harvesting of thousands of acres were planned to produce wheat, fruits and vegetables. In a single year General Vallejo harvested more than seventy thousand bushels of grain. His herds produced more than fifty thousand hides and immense quantities of tallow for trade with ships from New England beginning to come to the California coast.

Near the ranchhouse, shops and little factories of all kinds were established, with Indians trained to staff them. There was a tannery, gristmill, candle and soap works, a saddlery and cobbler shop and a blacksmith shop.

The huge, rambling adobe ranch house near Petaluma, the largest in the country, was the home of General Mariano Vallejo, the last of California's Mexican-Spanish governors. *Photograph: Courtesy Redwood Empire.*

Almost self-contained and self-sufficient, the ranch with its adobe house was the largest and most successful in a region where big ranches were commonplace.

In the summer of 1835, while the Petaluma Adobe was being developed, General Vallejo took time to found the Pueblo of Sonoma and laid out an eight-acre plaza, the largest in California. There he built a barracks for his troops, who drilled in the big plaza.

While living in Sonoma, General Vallejo was an unwilling spectator at a curious California event, the abortive Bear Flag Revolt (the revolt of the local citizens against Mexican rule) in the summer of 1846, ten weeks after the general had advocated the annexation of California to the United States. A prisoner in his own home he watched the raising of the red, green and white flag with its star and grizzly bear (now official flag of California) over the Sonoma barracks, replacing the flag of Mexico. The Bear flag flew for a few weeks, and was replaced by the flag of the United States on July ninth.

Soon after that the Petaluma ranch had about fulfilled its purpose as a buttress against Russian encroachment and as a factor in the settlement of the northern California wilderness. In time General Vallejo sold the ranch for $25,000 and moved to a new and different type of house near Sonoma. The heirs of the purchaser, William D. Bliss, finally turned the adobe ranch house over to the state of California, which made it a state historical monument and restored it to the period of its greatest activity, about 1845.

Visitors to the adobe now see it as it was at that time, probably the finest and largest example of California adobe construction of the late Spanish and Mexican periods. It is not difficult to imagine the house as a teeming center of ranch life, the railings of the balcony hung with the finished weaving from ranch looms, stores piled under the shelter of the wide balcony eaves, festoons of peppers hung from the beams and rooms of the adobe set with the heavy but graceful furniture of Spanish ranch life.

It would be hard to imagine greater contrast between Petaluma Adobe and the second historic house General Vallejo built in 1850 on the western outskirts of Sonoma. It is a Victorian-Gothic frame house, with steep pitched roof and narrow dormer windows. Unusual features include a big gothic window in the second story and a lacy fringe of scroll-saw decorations festooning the eaves. More characteristic of the Atlantic seaboard at the time of its building than of pioneer California, the house was given an odd and romantic name by General Vallejo—"Lachryma Montis," a Latinized translation of the Indian name *Chiucuym*, meaning "tear of the mountain," because hot and cold springs gushed from the hills just north.

The new house was set in twenty carefully landscaped acres that were as Victorian in style as the house itself, with formal flower beds, carefully pruned trees and hedges and cast-iron animals scattered over the lawn. The house itself was built of redwood from forests to the north and, for insulation, adobe bricks were tucked between the walls. Near his home the general built a barnlike storehouse, now called the Swiss Chalet, using precut timbers shipped around the Horn, and bricks that had been ballast in sail-

In 1834, a Spanish outpost against the Russian colonists was built. The adobe style ranch house was the official residence of General Mariano Vallejo. *Photograph: Courtesy Redwood Empire.*

The spacious ranch house central patio was a center for ranch activities, and a training headquarters for Indians. *Photograph: Courtesy Redwood Empire.*

Lachryma Montis ("tear of
the mountain") a Victorian-
Gothic mansion, built in
1850 at Sonoma, California.
*Photograph: Courtesy
Redwood Empire.*

Cast-iron fountains and picket
fences accent the Victorian
style of the house.
*Photograph: Courtesy
Redwood Empire.*

ing ships. The storehouse was used to store wines, olives and other products from the general's ranch and farm lands. A granary on the second floor was sometimes used to house extra overnight guests who could not be accommodated in the main house.

During California's development under United States rule the general was an important man, and a popular one. He was active in politics, and was one of the members of the California constitutional convention in 1849. He helped establish Sonoma as the first county seat in California, with himself the first senator in the state legislature from the Sonoma district. He set aside part of his land holdings on Pablo Bay to the south as a site for a state capital. The community, called Vallejo, was the nominal capital of the state from 1851 to 1854, after which the capital was moved to Sacramento.

General Vallejo lived with his family at Lachryma Montis until 1890, when he died almost impoverished, his once great holdings frittered away to maintain a political and social position as one of California's most celebrated native sons.

In acquiring Lachryma Montis the state of California restored and refurnished it, using many Vallejo family possessions, so that it is seen today about as it was when the general and his family lived there. It is one of the few Victorian mansions in northern California, made distinctive by a unique collection of souvenirs gathered in a lifetime of service to two governments.

The two remarkable houses now preserved as state historical monuments are only a few miles apart in Sonoma County. The Petaluma Adobe should be visited first. It is about four miles east of Petaluma, off US 101 on Adobe Road. Lachryma Montis is a few miles farther east, the two towns linked by California 116, with the house on West Street just outside of the Sonoma town limits. Both houses are within fifty miles of San Francisco.

III

SETTLERS OF THE EASTERN SEABOARD

Spain had the first settlements in the New World, but colonists from other nations were not far behind. Starting in 1607 with the English settlement of Jamestown, Virginia, emigrants from several nations established settlements between Maine and Florida: the English in Virginia, New England, the Carolinas and Pennsylvania, and along Chesapeake Bay; the Dutch along the Hudson River; and the Swedish in Delaware.

Settlers of the Eastern Seaboard had quite different objectives than did the Spanish settlers in the West who cared little about clearing and cultivating the land. On the Atlantic shore of the New World, where settlements were based on royal grants of land, the colonists sought to tame a wilderness and convert forests into productive fields. Within a remarkably few years after the settlement of Jamestown, villages had grown to prosperous towns and the rich soil along tidal rivers was producing valuable crops that found eager markets across the seas.

Soon England took over Swedish and Dutch colonies in a bloodless expansion of her sovereignty and established colonial capitals in growing centers such as Boston, New York, Philadelphia, Baltimore and Williamsburg. Where once were forests now stood manorial estates and plantations that soon began sending a rising tide of agricultural wealth to their mother country: forest products, rice, wheat, indigo and chiefly tobacco—a New World miracle crop that in a few decades made plantation owners rich.

Some of the houses built by the harvests of the New World are still there, splendid monuments to a way of life that was almost unique in its day. Some became the ancestral homes of celebrated families. In two houses future Presidents of the United States were born. In a special sense the story of the development of the Eastern Seaboard is told in the proud houses that face the Hudson, the Potomac and the James rivers. A selection of some of the most interesting and remarkable of these truly historic homes is presented in the following pages, along with the stories of the families who lived in them.

Van Cortlandt Manor, Croton-on-Hudson, New York

The story of the Van Cortlandt family from Holland in the New World is a classic prototype of the American dream. The story begins with Oloff Van Cortlandt, who came to New Amsterdam in 1638 as a soldier of the Dutch West India Company. Ten years later he left the company to go into business for himself. He quickly began to achieve wealth and fame as a merchant, brewer and politician. He was one of the Dutch burgers who negotiated the surrender of New Amsterdam to the British in 1664 and later he became deputy mayor of New York.

Late in the seventeenth century Oloff's son Stephanus established the manor of Cortlandt, a vast wilderness estate of more than eighty thousand acres, extending ten miles along the east bank of the Hudson River, and twenty miles inland. The only building on the land was a stone hunting lodge used as a trading center for furs brought in by Indians, who in exchange for their claim to the land received a payment of "8 guns, 5 coats, 9 blankets, 14 fathoms of duffles [a rough cloth], 14 kettles, 12 shirts, 50 pounds of powder, 30 bars of lead, 18 hatchets, 18 hoes, 40 fathoms of black wampum, 80 fathoms white wampum, 2 ankers rum [about 20 gallons], 5 half vats strong beer, 6 earthen jugs, 14 knives, a small coat, 6 fathoms stroud cloth, 6 pairs stockings, 6 tobacco boxes."

In the next few years Van Cortlandt continued to acquire land and by 1697 the estate reached its greatest size, about two hundred square miles. In that year, in recognition of Stephanus Van Cortlandt's many civic and political activities, including a term as Mayor of New York, King William III issued a royal patent designating the vast estate as the "Lordship and Manor of Cortlandt."

Though most of his land was forest wilderness, the grant gave Van Cortlandt, then forty-four years old, special privileges: He had absolute control over all fish and game found on the land, a matter of importance since the land was rich in both. He could clear the forest and convert it to lumber, lease land to tenant settlers, hold court and try petty crimes. He was the patron of any church established on the land. His grant provided that as lord of the manor he would have one seat in the provincial assembly. For his rights he was to pay the King's governor forty shillings a year.

From that time on the manor began to develop from a primitive tract to a busy farm estate, and the original stone cabin grew to a spacious manor house, remaining in the Van Cortlandt family for 250 years.

As the estate gained fame so did members of the Van Cortlandt family. Philip Van Cortlandt became a general in the Revolutionary Army. Stephanus, the estate's founder, became Chief Justice of the New York State Supreme Court.

The evolution of the manor house from a primitive stone cabin into a fine big farmhouse and the acres of wilderness from forested hills into productive farm lands took many years, with most of the development occurring during the ownership of Pierre Van Cortlandt, grandson of the founder, Stephanus. He made the house the family home and lived there for sixty-seven years, until his death in 1814 at the age of ninety-three.

Within a few years after the manor had been created, construction of a second story began. Sandstone cut from quarries on the west bank of the Hudson River was ferried to the Van Cortlandt landing in the family's piragua, a two-masted workboat. The red and yellow brick seen in the house today probably came to the New World as ballast for ships. Timber from the family forests was cut in the family sawmill to make the roof beams and the wide, graceful porches that are part of the charm of the manor house today. As the house grew in comfort and size it was lived in more and more by the family, who sometimes came by horseback through the forests along the Hudson, but more often made the trip by water from the family town-house in New York.

The manor house was much more than a residence. It was the hub of a bustling community. Mills were built and flour sold to tenants who leased farms of from two hundred to two hundred fifty acres. (By 1718 there were ninety-one inhabitants living on manor land farms.)

The Van Cortlandt Manor, graceful and typically Dutch in design, was the ancestral home of the Van Cortlandt family. *Photograph: Courtesy Sleepy Hollow Restorations.*

Pierre's management was responsible for the handsome porches, for the plastering of interior walls, and for the fine furniture that is seen in the upper rooms today. He planted apple orchards, established a carpenter shop and blacksmith shop, a cowhouse and a beehouse. Clay from the family lands kept a brick kiln busy. There were sawmills and gristmills. At the family dock a schooner was tied up and used for trade up and down the Hudson.

On his land Pierre built roads and paths for horsemen. Before long there was enough traffic to require a ferry over the Croton River. The ferry, a scow, was moved across the river by a ferryman pulling on a rope anchored at each end. Since ferry owners were required by law to maintain resting places for travelers, a ferry house was built with sleeping quarters and an associated tavern that soon became a neighborhood gathering place.

Finally Pierre built a schoolhouse and hired a schoolmaster who was paid six pounds for four months of teaching a year. The eight Van Cortlandt children were pupils along with children from tenant families.

By the middle of the eighteenth century the manor was fully established. The manor house and associated grounds and buildings probably appeared much as visitors see them today. Life was busy, peaceful and prosperous; interrupted, gradually at first, then decisively, by the Revolutionary War. Members of the family played active parts, both military and political, in that war and in a sense the manor too went to war. It stirred with visitors on revolutionary business. One of them was Benjamin Franklin, and there is a family tradition that George Washington, during the retreat from New York after the Battle of White Plains, spent a night in the manor ferry house. But during most of the war the manor was a no man's land, caught between troop movements up and down the river. The family moved to Peekskill, New York, leaving the manor house deserted. During these years it was plundered by wandering soldiers. Inspecting it after the war, Pierre reported that vandals had stolen nearly all the doors, shutters and shelves from the house, timbers from the barn, cowhouse and beehouse, beds, chairs "and a great number of other furniture that cannot be recollected."

Pierre and his wife remained in Peekskill for several years, leaving his son, General Philip Van Cortlandt, to return to the manor house, repair war damages, and reestablish the business of the manor lands.

In the years that followed the manor came to full maturity. The big house, mellowed with the years, was fully repaired and refurnished. The original stone cabin on the ground floor was converted to a huge kitchen, where the family slaves attended spits and kettles, fetched wood from the woodpile, water from the well, and hams from the smokehouse. (On Pierre's death in 1814, all slaves were freed except one deemed too old to take care of herself.)

Following the Revolutionary War the manor lands, divided among various heirs, were completely settled by a farming population. A tax report of 1779 shows that 550 taxpayers lived on the land, presumably most of them tenant farmers.

Van Cortlandt enterprises prospered. There were busy flour- and saw-mills on both sides of the Croton River. Sailing ships piled high with barrels of flour and stacks of lumber, came and went from family docks. The extensive carefully cultivated family orchards and gardens provided variety and abundance for the family table.

Following 1784, a once-a-month round trip by "stage waggen" over the Albany Post road gave new life to the ferry house, a regular overnight stop for the trip.

The golden age of the manor ended, in a sense, with the death of Philip in 1831, though the house remained the home of his heirs until 1945, when it was sold outside the family for the first time in 250 years. In 1953 John D. Rockefeller, Jr., bought the house and five acres of land associated with it, and began restoring it to its condition at the height of the Pierre and Philip Van Cortlandt ownership.

Years of research and reconstruction have re-created an outstanding example of a Hudson Valley estate of the late eighteenth century and the restoration is considered the most perfect in the country. The house and immediate grounds now extend to about twenty acres and look as they probably did during the eighteenth century, except for one difference. During that period the Croton River was a considerable stream, wide and deep enough to require a ferry and to service good-sized ships. Recent damming to create the Croton Reservoir to the east has reduced the flow to little more than a minor stream. The highway that once served the ferry house and ferry has also been rerouted.

Van Cortlandt Manor, thanks to the restoration and the superb maintenance established by the Sleepy Hollow Foundation, which manages the property, is increasingly visited by travelers to the Hudson Valley. Entrance to the grounds is off Route 9, on Croton Point Avenue, then south on South Riverside Avenue, just south of the community of Croton-on-Hudson. The chief focus of interest is, of course, the manor house itself, with its graceful roof, wide second-story porches extending along the south front and on west and east sides. The manor's main entrance on the south is reached by flights of double steps from the lower level. Many visitors find that exploring the gardens and grounds before entering the manor house sets a mood. Such an exploration would include strolling down the brick-paved Long Walk connecting the manor with the Ferry House Tavern. Wide flower beds border the walk with Scotch roses and yellow poppies in bloom there in season, as well as direct descendants of plants Joanna, Pierre Van Cortland's wife, brought to the manor in 1749. South of the Long Walk are remnants of the family kitchen garden. North, behind a stone terrace wall is an orchard with apple and pear trees, the estate office and various outbuildings.

The manor house faces toward Manhattan, overlooking the Croton River and a wide stretch of the Hudson River. Wandering through its rooms evokes two centuries of family life. The lower floor, sturdy, massive and simple is the oldest part of the house and dates from the seventeenth cen-

tury. The upper floors reflect the grace and elegance of the eighteenth and early nineteenth centuries. They are set with handsome classical furniture and innumerable heirlooms of family life. Rooms of special interest include the dining room, with fine examples of Duncan Phyfe and William and Mary furniture. There, visiting members of the family and the landed aristocracy of the Hudson River Valley, as well as personages both political and military, were entertained with lavish hospitality.

Across a wide hall is the parlor, with handsome pieces of Chippendale and Queen Anne furniture. At the rear of the house is a bedroom with a curious name, the Prophet's Chamber, where circuit riders, ministers and bishops sometimes slept. Vivid notes of reality are innumerable small personal possessions scattered throughout the upper-story bedrooms.

Most visitors are fascinated by the lower floor of the manor house,

▷

The transition room of the Van Cortlandt Manor is the old parlor characteristic of the mid-eighteenth century. *Photograph: Courtesy Sleepy Hollow Restorations.*

Through the years, the
Van Cortlandt Manor became
more elegant as the fine furniture
suggestive of the late eighteenth
century was acquired. *Photograph:
Courtesy Sleepy Hollow Restorations.*

The brick Long Walk,
bordered with flowers, linked
the manor house of the Van
Cortlandt estate with the
ferry house. *Photograph:
Courtesy Sleepy Hollow
Restorations.*

The most fascinating room of the Van Cortlandt Manor is the old kitchen, with its big cooking fireplace and its walls hung with gleaming pewter and copper utensils.
Photograph: Courtesy Sleepy Hollow Restorations.

which was developed from the original stone house on the site. Its chief room is the huge kitchen, with its vast fireplace, beehive oven, turning spits, gleaming copper and pewter pots and pans. Beyond the kitchen is the milk room and an original family parlor. Some distance behind the house are the smokehouse and the "necessary house," or privy.

The ferry house and adjoining ferry house kitchen at the end of the Long Walk are faithful restorations of Dutch buildings after 1640 in the Hudson Valley. All cooking for ferry passengers was done in the kitchen; dining, sleeping, and diversion in the adjoining ferry house. Dormitory rooms were on the second floor, a tap room, gaming room and common room on the ground floor, all now refurnished and equipped with primitive country-style pieces including beds, tables and a notable collection of eighteenth-century pewter. The original ferry dock has been reconstructed, and the big bell on a high post in front of the ferry house that announced the imminent crossing of the ferry can be clanged today by visitors young and old.

Standing beside the bell post, hearing the peal of the big bell, one can easily conjure up the wider river spanned by a sagging rope, a large scow on the far shore loaded with a "stage waggen" hitched to weary horses, and

filled with tired and dusty passengers, who in a few minutes would quench their thirst and rest in the Van Cortlandt ferry house.

Philipsburg Manor, Upper Mills, New York

There is a fascinating parallel between the lives and achievement of Oloff Van Cortlandt, father of the founder of Van Cortlandt Manor, and Frederick Philipse, who is believed to have sailed to New Amsterdam at about the same time that Peter Stuyvesant became Dutch governor of the colony. Philipse was a carpenter and for a time worked for the governor.

The parallel begins with the careers of both men in the New World. Within a few years the two had become wealthy and owned vast tracts of forest wilderness north of Manhattan. Both became politically influential and became involved in extensive and highly profitable commercial enterprises.

The two manor estates adjoined each other. Philipsburg Manor was on the Pocantico River, near its junction with the Hudson, a few miles to the south.

For about a hundred years the Van Cortlandt and Philipse families, associated by marriage and in business, were close neighbors. There the parallel ends.

During the Revolutionary War the Van Cortlandt family produced great patriots, political and military leaders, who with the war's end went on to become leading members of the Hudson Valley aristocracy, maintaining their manor house as a family home until recent years.

Not so the Philipse family. Its heirs, owners of the manor estate on the Hudson, chose to support the Crown in the war, were denounced as traitors and forced into exile. The estate, sold at auction, was divided and the historic manor house, once the core of a vast, unique and prosperous enterprise, favorite home of one of the richest men in the New World, passed through many hands and many modifications.

This is the story of that remarkable house, the man who built it and the enterprises associated with it.

Frederick Philipse was born in the Dutch village of Bolswaert in 1626, the same year that Peter Minuit, director general of New Netherlands bought Manhattan Island from the Indians. Young Philipse became a carpenter, and as a carpenter, he is believed to have accompanied Peter Stuyvesant to the New World, where that stern and stubborn Dutchman became the governor of the colony. Working briefly for Peter Stuyvesant, Philipse soon became involved in many enterprises. He dabbled in real estate and soon owned assorted tracts of land and houses in Manhattan and nearby. He engaged in overseas trade, chartered vessels for the purpose and operated at least one ship of his own. But his most successful venture in those early years was marriage in 1662 to Margaret Hardenbroeck, one of the richest widows in the colony.

Margaret, like Frederick, had a flair for business, and together the couple extended their activities and holdings. Within twenty years, they owned, in addition to scattered parcels of land in Manhattan, Long Island and New Jersey, about one-third of what is now Westchester County in New York, about ninety thousand acres of land extending many miles north along the east bank of the Hudson River as far as the Croton River, east to the Bronx River. In the meantime the industrious couple had extended their shipping interests, with Philipse vessels seen in most ports of the Western world. They carried furs, whale oil and tobacco to England from New York and Virginia; sugar, cocoa, sassafras and logwood from the West Indies; lumber from the colonies to the West Indies; manufactured goods from England to the colonies; and from Africa brought spices, ivory and slaves to the New World.

But with all his business and commercial activities Frederick did not neglect social and political opportunities. He saw to it that his stepdaughter, Margaret's child by her first marriage, married into the rich and socially prominent Van Cortlandt family. In 1674 Frederick was made an alderman by Governor Andros, and next year a member of the Governor's Council, a post he held until 1698. Records of Manhattan as early as 1674 show Philipse to be the richest man in the city.

But he was to become richer. His land, his first love, helped make him so. The vast estate he had put together along the Hudson from a series of purchases, all from Indian owners, was in the beginning heavily forested wilderness. But it was splendid and beautiful wilderness, some of the finest land in the New World. Rolling, wooded hills dropped down to the wide channel of the Hudson. From the hills streams meandered west to the great river, forming a series of coves and channels.

A particular cove, made by the winding channel of the Pocantico River, caught Frederick's special fancy. He saw it as a site for a trading center and as a base for manufacturing, where the products of the land could be converted into lumber and flour, and where furs brought in for trading could be loaded on Philipse vessels. There was also stone to be quarried, and as the land was cleared and converted to farms, tenants of the land could form a captive market for goods made abroad and brought to the New World in Philipse vessels.

Early Dutch settlers called Frederick's favorite cove Die Slapering Haven, which Washington Irving, who was to live nearby, translated into a name that would become famous around the world: Sleepy Hollow.

As his plans developed, Philipse called his estate on the Pocantico Upper Mills, to distinguish it from another project in Yonkers several miles to the south called Lower Mills. Construction of the buildings and facilities of the Upper Mills complex began about 1680, with most of the materials derived from Philipse land. A log dam in the Pocantico River created a mill pond to power an overshot water wheel that turned the stones of a gristmill, with a wharf below it, where specially built Hudson River sloops could receive their cargoes of flour, lumber and furs.

Just behind the mill Philipse built a two-story stone house from rough-hewn blocks of native stone and fieldstone. The ground floor was a kitchen and storage cellar cut into a bank. Two upper floors, the family living quarters, were one room wide and two rooms deep. A huge single chimney, serving several fireplaces, rose through the center of the house.

Frederick Philipse could easily have afforded an elegant mansion, but chose a simple, relatively small, almost austere house, furnished with the sturdy Dutch country furniture typical of the period.

The industrious Margaret, mother of Frederick's four children, died about 1692, too soon to share Frederick's greatest honor, capstone of his prosperous career. In 1693 the reigning English monarchs, William and Mary, granted a royal patent or charter to Frederick Philipse creating the "Lordship or Manor of Philipseborough," stipulating the lands involved, making Frederick one of the largest landholders in America, and his simple stone house on the banks of the Pocantico River a manor house.

Soon after the death of Margaret, Frederick, in his mid-sixties, married another widow, Catherine, the daughter of Oloff Stevense Van Cortlandt, Frederick's neighbor to the north. It was chiefly on Catherine's account that Frederick built a church in 1697, about 150 yards from his manor house. Made of rough stone the little church has a tiny steeple holding a bell cast in Holland; just above is a weathervane with Frederick Philipse's symbol in

Typically Dutch in every detail are the furniture and decorations of an upper room of Philipsburg Manor. Photograph: Courtesy Sleepy Hollow Restorations.

Philipsburg Manor has been
superbly restored. The estate's
manor house, gristmill, dam
and mill wheel appear as they
were during the heyday of the
estate's activity, about 250
years ago. *Photograph:
Courtesy Sleepy Hollow
Restorations.*

The manor house of the Philipsburg estate on the Hudson began to develop about 1680 and never lost its austere, roughhewn and primitive look. *Photograph: Courtesy Sleepy Hollow Restorations.*

the shape of a flag. Various relics still used in the church bear the name of Frederick and his wife Catherine. Years later it became known as the Old Dutch Church of Sleepy Hollow, that Washington Irving helped make famous. Most visitors who explore the present restoration of Philipsburg Manor walk across the highway flanking the restored area to find fascination in the church and the ancient burying ground around it.

Frederick Philipse was seventy-six years old when he died in 1702, and his son, Adolph, inherited Upper Mills. The younger Philipse was thirty-seven years old and one of the busiest men in New York, a member of the King's Council, a judge of the Supreme Court, a representative in the Assembly and a highway commissioner of Westchester County. But with all his interests he kept an eye on Upper Mills, carefully maintaining and extending it. Among other things he added a third set of millstones. And about 1720 he doubled the size of the manor house by duplicating the original plan, giving each main floor four instead of two rooms. In the liv-

As the Philipse family became increasingly important members of the Dutch Hudson River aristocracy, touches of elegance and sophistication were added to the manor house, suggested by this upper floor dining room. *Photograph: Courtesy Sleepy Hollow Restorations.*

▷

The big Dutch kitchen of the manor house of the Philipsburg estate looks as it did in the late seventeenth century. *Photograph: Courtesy Sleepy Hollow Restorations.*

ing quarters for the family he added furniture of grace and elegance. Under Adolph's management the tenant population grew from two hundred in 1702 to eleven hundred in 1750, the year he died.

With Adolph's death the vast estate was inherited by his nephew, Frederick II, who died a year later leaving the estate to his son, Frederick III. This great-grandson of the estate's founder lost no time in disposing of the property, leasing Upper Mills to a farmer. Rents from his lands kept him in luxury in his Yonkers mansion. With the onset of the Revolutionary War Frederick III elected to support the English Crown, and for his activities was charged with treason and his property confiscated. While he lay dying in England his confiscated manor lands were put up for sale by the state, to be sold at auction.

The house and its lands were sold many times until in 1940 the holdings were acquired by John D. Rockeller, Jr., with the object of restoring the property to its appearance between 1720 and 1750. Many years of meticulous historical and archaeological investigation began, followed by a program of restoration that continued until the superbly authentic result was opened to the public in the summer of 1969.

Visitors can now see a unique restoration of early American history: a manor house with its period furniture, and a water-powered gristmill behind a millpond with an adjoining wharf.

Few restorations in the country are more fascinating, creating with vivid accuracy a fragment of colonial life of 250 years ago. The restoration is just north of Tarrytown, with an entrance leading to a parking lot and Visitor Center west of US 9.

Berkeley Plantation, Virginia

As rivers of the country go the James River in Virginia doesn't amount to much. Only 340 miles long it becomes an independent river in the mountains of western Virginia to break through the fall line of the Blue Ridge Mountains near Richmond, where it becomes navigable. Steadily widening it soon becomes a broad tidal estuary, losing itself in the vast harbor of Hampton Roads. Its character is similar to that of other rivers that flow east and southeast into Chesapeake Bay: the Potomac, the York, the Rappahannock. Together they create the remarkable region called Tidewater, where more historic events occurred, and where more historic homes exist than anywhere else in the country.

Among Virginia's tidal rivers none is richer in history than the James. On its northern bank, in 1607, the redoubtable Captain John Smith and his followers established the first permanent English settlement in America, and promptly became responsible for a series of other firsts—the first tobacco grown in the New World, the first glass, the first legislative assembly. Jamestown spawned the splendid colonial capital of Virginia, Williamsburg, a few miles north of Jamestown. The tobacco first grown at Jamestown accounted for the establishment of a chain of plantations on the north bank of the

James that prospered greatly. Plantation owners became rich and built handsome manor houses, some of which are the finest in Virginia.

Among the plantations on the James is Berkeley, thirty miles from Williamsburg, twenty-five miles from Richmond. Other plantations are larger, and some have bigger and finer mansions, but in historic association none approaches Berkeley. A remarkable series of events took place there. The ancestral home of two Presidents of the United States, it was also the site of the first official Thanksgiving celebration in America. The first whisky distilled in the New World was made at Berkeley. A Berkeley owner established the first shipyard and shipbuilding industry in the country. Berkeley owners included a signer of the Declaration of Independence, several governors of Virginia, and, during the Civil War, with the army of General McClellan quartered on Berkeley land, a Union general wrote that most moving of all bugle calls, "Taps."

The story of Berkeley begins in 1619 when King James I granted a big tract of Virginia to five cousins from Berkeley Castle. On December 5, 1619, only twelve years after the founding of Jamestown, forty-three settlers arrived in the ship *Marget* to take over their grant, Berkeley Hundred. On coming ashore they held the first official Thanksgiving ceremony in the New World.

Three years later there occurred a most unusual event, the successful distillation of whisky made from Berkeley corn, called bourbon. The distiller was an Anglican priest. In the files of the present owner of Berkeley there is a fascinating letter written by the cleric to friends in England recounting euphoric results from drinking his brew, reporting that those who did so usually forgot the hardships of the New World.

Toward the end of the seventeenth century part of the vast tract granted to the original Berkeley settlers was acquired by the aristocratic Harrison family of Virginia. Benjamin Harrison III moved to the land and began to develop the area now included in the present plantation. One of his first projects was an extensive shipyard, with drydock, wharves and warehouses—the first in Virginia. It was probably completed about 1700 and was known for many years as Harrison's Landing. Rotted pilings in the James River near the shore at Berkeley are all that now is left of it.

In 1710 Benjamin Harrison III died and the estate passed to his widow and ten-year-old son, Benjamin Harrison IV, whose major contribution to the plantation was the building of a handsome manor house. Berkeley today looks as it did when completed in 1726. It is the oldest three-story brick

▷

Built in 1726, historic Berkeley on the James is classically Georgian in design, and was the ancestral home of two Presidents of the United States. *Photograph: Courtesy Virginia State Travel Service.*

The First Thanksgiving

It became necessary to strengthen the ranks of the early Virginia Colonies, as homesickness, famine and disease had taken their frightful toll.

Thus in the year 1619 a small band of men landed here and gave thanks to Almighty God. In the years to follow "Berkeley and Hundred" became a thriving community.

On the night of March 22, 1622 the entire colony was wiped out by Indians. History records that Berkeley was abandoned, but it also testifies that this same spirit waxed stronger in the hearts of countless men to follow, to make this land safe and free, free to bring forth the fruits in greater abundance. Math 21:43

May we ever show thanks to our Creator for this heritage by increasing it.

house in Virginia. Classically Georgian in design, it was simpler and somewhat more austere than later Tidewater mansions. It became the principal home of the Harrison family for more than a hundred years.

When the builder of Berkeley Mansion died at the age of forty-five, his eighteen-year-old son, then a student at the College of William and Mary in Williamsburg, took over the plantation. Most illustrious of the Benjamin Harrisons, fifth in the family succession, he was a signer of the Declaration of Independence, three times governor of Virginia, and was the owner of five other plantations in the Tidewater region in addition to Berkeley.

But Benjamin Harrison V has even more of a claim to fame because, in 1773, a son, William Henry Harrison, was born at Berkeley. He was to become the ninth President of the United States and grandfather of Benjamin Harrison, the twenty-third President. Benjamin Harrison was regarded as a maverick Harrison in the eyes of his relatives because he was not born at Berkeley, or even in Virginia. His birthplace was Ohio, part of the frontier region his grandfather, the ninth President, had helped settle and develop as governor of the Indiana Territory.

William Henry Harrison, who won national fame as an Indian fighter, served only briefly as President. On April 4, 1841, thirty-one days after delivering an inaugural address (written at Berkeley), he died of pneumonia.

Twenty-one years after the death of President Harrison the last historic event associated with Berkeley Plantation occurred. In July, 1862, after seven days of fighting before Richmond, General McClelland, Commander of the Army of the Potomac, took over the plantation, made Berkeley Manor his headquarters and quartered most of his army on the plantation grounds. One of his staff was General Daniel Butterfield, who, on the back of an envelope, wrote the music for a bugle call, then whistled it to Bugler Oliver Norton, who for the first time played the short, solemn and deeply moving "Taps."

Berkeley today, said to be visited by more people than any other plantation on the James, is seen as it was during its last years as the Harrison family home, thanks to its present owner, Malcolm Jamieson. Jamieson's ownership of the plantation came about in a curious way. His father, born in Scotland in 1851, was brought to the New World with his family. During the Civil War he enlisted as a drummer boy with the Union Army, serving with the Army of the Potomac. In 1862 he was among the troops camped on Berkeley grounds, and perhaps even heard "Taps" played for the first time.

Years later, on a lumber-buying trip, Jamieson returned to the region of Berkeley and bought the manor house and many surrounding acres. His son, now in residence at Berkeley, divides his time between operating the plantation and restoring the mansion and grounds, and has been highly successful. The fourteen hundred plantation acres produce barley (exported for German beer), wheat, corn and soybeans. Sheep and cattle graze on the pastures; the sheep also close-crop the wide lawn around the mansion. In addition, Jamieson maintains an extensive aviary and a plantation of boxwood, selling both honey and small box plants to visitors. He has considered reviving Berkeley distilling.

To visit Berkeley, unless you arrive by water on the James River, one

First historic event to occur on the land of Berkeley Plantation was the celebration of Thanksgiving in 1619. *Photograph: Courtesy Virginia State Travel Service.*

must travel the river road, Virginia 5, which winds along through fields and forests just north of the river. On the south side of the highway are a succession of entrance gates to plantations that face the river. The gates of Berkeley are among them. A gravel drive leads south to the mansion, which is set among a grove of huge and ancient magnolia. The present mansion entrance is the original rear of the house which crowns a low bluff overlooking the river behind wide lawns. All around are farm buildings, some former slave quarters, the original plantation kitchen and bachelor quarters. Boxwood, ancient and beautiful, grows all about. The restored plantation gardens lie between the mansion and the river, and scattered about are tablets and memorials that help tell the historic story of Berkeley.

More of the story lies within the house, the lower floor of which is open to visitors who can see beautiful restored colonial furniture, Harrison originals or other pieces very like them. Books, pictures, maps and old documents

Classically elegant, the dining room of the Berkeley Plantation exhibits furniture owned by three generations of the Harrison family. Photograph: Courtesy Virginia State Travel Service.

Some of the Harrison portraits
and possessions that grace the
Great Room of the Berkeley
Plantation. *Photograph:
Courtesy Virginia State
Travel Service.*

fill in the details. There is a family burial plot, carefully maintained by Malcolm Jamieson, where generations of Harrisons lie buried.

Stratford Hall, Robert E. Lee Birthplace, Virginia

In several ways Stratford Hall, overlooking the Potomac River from high wooded bluffs, is unusual. It was the birthplace and home of more renowned Americans than any dwellings in the country. It is one of the finest examples of early Georgian design, with some unique architectural features. And, restored, it is an almost perfect example of a big colonial plantation with characteristic industries and plants.

Stratford derives its chief renown from the fact that Robert E. Lee, one of the world's finest soldiers, commander of the Confederate Armies during the Civil War, was born there. But other famous men were born and lived at Stratford and preceded Lee—three generations of them. They were all members of the renowned Lee family, probably the single most distinguished family of Colonial America. Stratford dwellers included twelve burgesses of Virginia, four members of the Virginia Convention of 1776, the first native-born Virginian to become governor of Virginia plus three more governors of Virginia; two signers of the Declaration of Independence; members of the

66

Continental Congress; and distinguished military leaders of both the Revolutionary and Civil wars.

Stratford began with a patent granted to Thomas Pope, one of George Washington's great-great-grandfathers, in 1651. The patent covered more than twelve hundred acres of high land on the south bank of the Potomac, a superb tract with many great forest trees. It was first called Cliffs Plantation, because of its location at the crest of the Nomini Cliffs. The estate was purchased in 1716 by Colonel Thomas Lee, but he did not begin construction of the present baronial mansion until 1729. It was completed about three years later.

Whether Colonel Lee himself was responsible for the design of the house, or whether he engaged architectural assistance, is not known, but the result was a near masterpiece. Simple and robust in style the great house has impressive, almost austere dignity. It is also superbly symmetrical, built on an H plan, derived from Elizabethan and Jacobean times. The vertical sides of the H are identical wings, each sixty feet long and thirty feet wide. Between them, comprising the bar of the H, is a great central hall, thirty by thirty feet. There are twenty rooms in the two stories of the house, under a wide-eaved roof sloping from all sides to H-shaped ridge poles that support two arcaded clusters of four chimneys. They are the mansion's most distinctive architectural feature, one group rising at the center of each wing. All buildings of the estate are of finely colored native Virginia brick. In the mansion itself the brick is laid in Flemish bond to form a striking checkered pattern. The south and east entrances, almost a full story above the ground, are reached by graceful flights of steps.

The mansion stands at the center of a rectangle with four single-story dependencies near each corner of the main house. One was used as Colonel Lee's law office and library; another was a big kitchen with an adjoining smokehouse that had a fireplace large enough to accommodate a roasting ox. Just west of Colonel Lee's office was a big brick stable, home of the fine horses that all horse-loving Lees rode. Beyond the kitchen was a kitchen garden which adjoined an extensive formal garden with box-bordered beds and a box maze. From the area of the mansion two roads lead north toward the Potomac River, one to the crest of the cliffs and one down to the ledge of the river where Colonel Lee maintained the estate landing. There ships, some owned by Colonel Lee, brought furniture, silk, tea, wine and other cargoes to be exchanged for estate products, chiefly tobacco. Near the "warff" was the plantation store, tobacco warehouses, a shipyard and cooper shop.

From early times, sheep have close-cropped the wide lawns of the Berkeley Plantation, the oldest three-story brick house in Virginia. *Photograph: Courtesy Virginia State Travel Service.*

▷

Stratford Hall on the Potomac, the ancestral home of Virginia's renowned Lee family, is one of the finest surviving examples of a complete, working colonial plantation. *Photograph: Courtesy Virginia State Travel Service.*

Not far away were the estate gristmill and sawmill. More than most plantations in colonial times Stratford was almost self-contained and self-sufficient.

Colonel Thomas Lee completed his big estate and mansion about 1732, and lived there until his death in 1750 at the age of sixty. He had eleven children, eight of them sons, four of whom were born at Stratford. They included Thomas Henry Lee and Francis Lightfoot Lee, both distinguished soldiers and signers of the Declaration of Independence. The room where they were born, a bedroom at the front on the right, is of special interest to visitors of Stratford today. For in that room, Robert Edward Lee was born on January 19, 1807. The future general's father was the great-grandson of the estate's founder, Thomas Lee, and son of General Henry (Light Horse Harry) Lee. His mother was Ann Hill Carter, member of another famed Virginia family.

Though he lived at Stratford only as a boy, General Lee returned to visit it many times, and wrote vivid descriptions of the splendid life of the estate, a pinnacle of colonial cultural, social and plantation life, maintained with gay and leisured elegance.

"The owner lived here in great state," he wrote, and to a young woman who had sent him a photograph of a painting of Stratford, he wrote that the picture "recalls scenes of my earliest recollections and happiest days. Though unseen for years, every feature of the house is familiar to me . . . the approach to the house is on the south, along the side of a lawn several hundred acres

Authentically restored, the huge kitchen in one of several outbuildings of Stratford Hall was once the working center for a corps of the plantation's slaves. *Photograph:.Courtesy Virginia State Travel Service.*

in extent, adorned with cedars, oaks and forest poplars. On ascending a hill not far from the gate the traveler comes in full view of the mansion, when the road turns to the right and leads to a grove of sugar maples, around which it sweeps to the house." Two earlier reports of visitors mention fig trees at Stratford, as well as "vineyards, orangeries and lawns that surround the house."

Stratford appears today essentially as it was when Thomas Lee and his family lived there, thanks to two agencies, the Robert E. Lee Memorial Foundation and the Garden Club of Virginia. The Lee Foundation acquired the property in 1932, and began restoring it as a memorial to the Confederate commander. At about the same time the Garden Club took over the restoration of the grounds and gardens. Both efforts, now complete, have succeeded so splendidly that visitors see the great estate as a working demonstration of eighteenth-century plantation life. Cattle and horses again graze the wide fields. The estate mill grinds flour and meal, and Virginia hams hang in the smokehouse behind the huge kitchen, where the gear and utensils of colonial times seem ready for use.

The classic elegance of colonial life is suggested by spacious rooms of the mansion: the beautifully paneled thirty-foot-square great hall, with its sixteen-pronged chandelier and splendid examples of the best craftsmanship in fine English and American furniture of the period; the more intimate

Part of the cost of the rare and handsome furniture and china in the twin dining rooms of Stratford Hall was derived from a grant made by Queen Caroline of England, whose portrait hangs in the large main room. *Photograph: Courtesy Virginia State Travel Service.*

living quarters of the family including the handsome dining room with a rare Queen Anne table and family portraits. But more than any room, the "Mother's Room," with its high-posted canopied bed, evokes not only colonial life but suggests the special meaning of Stratford: home for more than two hundred years of one of the most illustrious families of America. Many Lee men were born in this room, the most illustrious of whom was the great General Robert E. Lee.

Stratford Hall and the estate grounds are open to visitors year round. The plantation, about ninety miles southeast of Washington and forty miles east of Fredericksburg, is on Virginia Highway 3. Because of the plantation's isolation, luncheon served in a special dining room is available to visitors between noon and 2 P.M., April 1 to October 31.

George Washington Birthplace, Virginia

Most visitors to Stratford Hall also stop to see the birthplace of George Washington, only a few miles west of the Lee birthplace on Virginia Highway 3, about thirty-eight miles southeast of Fredericksburg.

Many who visit the Washington birthplace are both puzzled and disappointed. The house bears no resemblance to the fine colonial mansion one might envision. It is one of the ironies of history that the house where the first President of the United States was born doesn't exist. It burned down on Christmas Day, 1779, and was never rebuilt. There are no records that give a clue to the size and character of the house. Nor has extensive investigation at the site discovered with certainty what might have been the foundations of the actual birthplace. But the general site is authentic and is now preserved as a national monument. The memorial mansion that visitors see today is intended to look like a plantation house where George Washington, the first child of Augustine and Mary Ball Washington, might have been born on February 22, 1732 (February 11 by the old-style calendar). It is in no sense a restoration or a reconstruction of a known house. It is intended to represent a Virginia plantation house of the eighteenth century, such a house as Augustine, who was not a rich man, might have built for himself after he acquired a relatively small plantation of 150 acres in 1718. The plantation, fronting on Pope's Creek, was a short distance south of the Potomac. Sometime between 1723 and 1725 Augustine hired a carpenter to build a small plantation house, which was probably completed in 1726.

Many visitors to the present Wakefield, the name the plantation came to be called, are surprised to see that the house has only eight rooms, none of them large, four downstairs and four tucked in under sloping eaves on the second floor. It looks like many other houses built in the Tidewater area of Virginia during the first half of the eighteenth century. Actually, the house is a typical colonial cottage, furnished with colonial furniture, though a tilt-top table in the dining room is believed to have been in the original house, perhaps at the time of Washington's birth.

But though a visit to the house and its extensive and beautifully restored grounds, including an ancient burying ground nearby where twenty-eight members of the Washington clan are buried, is something of a letdown, it is worthwhile in the sense that it vividly re-creates a link in the Washington story.

That story begins in the New World in 1658 when John Washington, great-great-grandfather of George, reached Virginia on the vessel *Seahorse of London,* sent to fetch a cargo of tobacco back to England. During a storm the ship ran aground and foundered in the Potomac River. John Washington, second officer, decided to stay in the New World. It was a wise move. Soon he married Anne Pope, daughter of a wealthy landowner who lived near Mattox Creek, not far from the present birthplace site. For a wedding

Believed to be a reasonable facsimile of the original George Washington birthplace, a handsome reconstruction of a typical colonial farmhouse dominates the original birthplace setting. *Photograph: Courtesy National Park Service.*

gift Colonel Pope gave the couple a seven hundred-acre tract overlooking the Potomac. In 1664 John Washington moved to a new house on his land. Successive generations of Washingtons were all successful plantation owners and civic leaders in Virginia, maintaining Tidewater plantations. John's son was Lawrence, George's grandfather. His son, George's father, Augustine, attended school in England as a boy and later attained a degree of wealth and influence, growing up on the family estate at Bridges Creek.

With land purchased in 1718, Augustine began to develop his own plantation and he maintained it for nine years. In 1735, three years after the birth of George, he moved to another family plantation at Hunting Creek, now known as Mount Vernon, and four years later moved again to Ferry Farm, on the east bank of the Rappahannock opposite Fredericksburg where George spent most of the years of his youth.

But other Washingtons continued to own and live at Wakefield. Upon Augustine's death, it passed to Augustine, Jr., half-brother of George. His son, William Augustine Washington, was living at Wakefield when it was destroyed by fire in 1779. Why the house was not rebuilt no one knows, but the land remained Washington property. The family graveyard was there, and near what is thought to have been the site of the house, the stark ruins of a kitchen chimney have stood for a hundred years.

Almost a century after the Wakefield house burned down, efforts were made to memorialize the birth site. In 1882, Washington heirs and the state of Virginia gave the family burying ground and a tract of eleven acres to the United States government. In 1923, the Wakefield National Memorial Association was organized to recover the birthplace grounds and make the site a shrine for the American people. Later, Congress authorized the building of a house that might resemble the colonial cottage where George Washington was born. The site, gradually extended to 394 acres and including most of the original Augustine Washington plantation, was made a national monument in 1930, the house erected the next year.

Things to see at the monument now include a curiously irrelevant granite shaft, a miniature Washington Monument, erected near the entrance by the federal government in 1896. Most important is the simulated birthplace house of handmade bricks from clay dug from an adjoining field, its design and furnishings like those of other modest plantation homes of the period. Near the house is a typical colonial-period kitchen. Visitors find interest in the carefully restored grounds. Many fine trees may have been there when Washington was born, and fig trees, herbs and flowers are doubtless descended from plants growing there when Washington was a little boy. A colonial garden near the house has boxwood more than one hundred years old, probably descended from original Wakefield boxwood. In the garden grow only flowers, vines, herbs and berries common to Virginia gardens of the period.

Wakefield is open to visitors year round, administered by the National Park Service. A two-mile entrance road connects the monument to Virginia Highway 3.

Huge old trees and ancient boxwood hedges were there when the actual birthplace of George Washington burned down, to be later replaced by a typical colonial farmhouse as a memorial. *Photograph: Courtesy National Park Service.*

Tryon Palace, New Bern, North Carolina

During the eighteenth century many mansions were built in Colonial America, chiefly in the Tidewater regions of southern states like Virginia and the Carolinas. Some were big and splendid, elegant manor houses of great plantation estates. But palaces, for which a dictionary definition is, "official residence of a sovereign or other exalted person," were rare. Two palaces were built in the colonies, in Virginia and adjoining North Carolina. Each was a home for a king's governor. Each was a dwelling of magnificence, superbly furnished with the finest examples of Georgian England's cabinet-makers, craftsmen and artists. Each was set in gardened grounds of unique beauty. And, before the end of the century, each palace had been destroyed by fire. And, finally, in our own time, each was magnificently rebuilt and restored.

The Virginia palace was the most famous and survived longer. It was built at Williamsburg in 1720. The fire that demolished it occurred in 1781. The Palace of Governors at Williamsburg, now one of the great showplaces of the country, was in a sense an impersonal mansion, serving as the home of a succession of governors both for the province and State of Virginia.

The North Carolina palace was at New Bern, and although it was the official residence of the King's royal governor for North Carolina, it was in a special sense a personal dwelling, and so is called Tryon Palace. William Tryon, governor of North Carolina, persuaded the English Government to provide him with an appropriate dwelling. He engaged an architect and builder, helped plan the palace, supervised its construction and contributed both his wealth and his possessions to furnishing it. Ironically, Governor Tryon lived only briefly in his magnificent new home. A year after it was completed he was transferred to New York.

In the spring of 1765, soon after succeeding Arthur Dobbs as royal governor of the province of North Carolina, William Tryon recommended to the Board of Trade in London that New Bern be made the permanent capital of the province. New Bern's location made it a logical choice. It was in the heart of the rich coastal Tidewater region of North Carolina, a seaport on the tidal estuary of the Neuse River, and about 150 miles south of the rival provincial capital of Virginia, the then busy, beautiful city of Williamsburg, where the Palace of Governors was widely regarded as the proudest of all the dwellings of colonial governors. No other official residence even approached it in elegance and splendor.

No doubt William Tryon, newly made governor of North Carolina, felt that his province deserved something to rival the Virginia palace. He lost no time in seeing that this was done. Within two months the colonial assembly of North Carolina had authorized five thousand pounds toward the project, Governor Tryon engaged John Hawks, master builder and professional architect who had come from England with Tryon, to design and build an appropriate capitol and dwelling. The appointment was apparently no surprise to Hawks, who must have been quietly working on plans for

Tryon Palace, built in 1770 at New Bern, North Carolina, has been superbly restored to its original elegance. Photograph: Courtesy North Carolina Department of Conservation.

some time. Six weeks after he was officially hired he had evaluations ready to submit to the Crown.

Hawks' plan was soon accepted and before the end of the summer of 1767 construction began. By the following March, Governor Tryon happily reported that "the body of the house is already carried up to the plates." The plans called for a thirty-eight room dwelling and combined capitol, classically Georgian in design, with a central brick house of two main stories, eighty-seven feet wide and fifty-seven feet deep. Two outlying wings, each of two low stories, were connected to the main building by graceful semicircular arcades. The combined palace-capitol was set among extensive grounds, within high brick walls. It would be like nothing else in North Carolina, or in all the colonies, for that matter.

Building the kind of palace the Hawks plan called for took a lot of doing, and money. Governor Tryon borrowed an additional ten thousand pounds from a prosperous local merchant at 8 percent interest. Presumably a local tax would eventually retire the loan. Hawks assembled the materials and the skilled labor required for the building from near and far. Craftsmen were brought in from Pennsylvania and New York. A specialist in metalwork was brought from England to fashion the elaborate gutters and downspouts the plan required. He used eight tons of imported lead doing so. Mantels for the many fireplaces of the great house, each individually carved, were brought from England, as were window frames and doors and much of the fine paneling. About all that was acquired locally were bricks. The most elaborate exterior detail of the great house was the ornately carved, colorful coat-of-arms of King George III, centered in the pediment of the façade, two stories above the main entrance.

While the exterior of the palace was handsome and classically correct in the best traditions of Georgian design, the interior was beautiful and splendid. With the possible exception of the Palace of Governors in Williamsburg, no other mansion in the colonies could match it in elegance. In a special sense the interior was the creation of Governor Tryon. He paid for much of it from his personal resources since the Privy Council, fearing that it would set an uncomfortable precedent, refused to grant funds needed for furniture, pictures, draperies and rugs. So the governor spent his own money for them with a lavish hand. The results were spectacular. The furniture, chiefly mahogany, was typically English designed and made by the best craftsmen of the period. For the walls the governor imported silk and damask draperies from Italy, and acquired fine portraits of the royal family and his own ancestors, along with landscapes by some of the best painters of the day. Mirrors, some massive, with elaborately carved and molded gilt frames, were everywhere throughout the downstairs rooms. A unique accessory in the huge council chamber was a massive, ornate musical and mechanical clock equipped with a repertoire of operatic tunes, said to be the first clock of its kind ever made.

Governor Tryon made a detailed inventory of all his personal possessions in the palace that in time would give great assistance to teams of experts involved in the future restoration.

Flowers and plants like those originally there again fill the intricately patterned, restored garden of Tryon Palace. *Photograph: Courtesy Tryon Palace Commission.*

Three years after building of the palace began it was finished and Governor Tryon, his wife, Margaret, and their nine-year-old daughter moved in. The palace had cost the equivalent of $75,000, and was certainly one of the most splendid buildings in Colonial America, a showplace for travelers, many calling it the most beautiful building in America. For about a year entertainment was lavish, gay and elegant, with guests attended by liveried servants and much candle-lit banqueting.

Then after a year Governor Tryon left his sumptuous house for New York, where he was named governor, taking with him all his personal possessions, and leaving the palace sparsely furnished for his successor, Josiah Martin, who lived there with his family until 1775. Then the whole region was flooded with a rising tide of revolution against the King.

The subsequent history of Tryon's Palace was sad. It became increasingly shabby and rundown, though the building served as the first state capitol of North Carolina. Occasionally it was a setting for festive events, such as a ball tendered to George Washington in 1791. Then his horse was stabled in the former executive offices. In writing of his visit later President Washington described the palace as "a good brick building now hastening to ruin." The ruin progressed steadily, reached a climax of destruction in 1798, when a black woman, carrying a torch to hunt for eggs in the basement, started a fire that destroyed the central building. The west wing, not burned, subsequently served as a warehouse, dwelling, stable, carriage house, parochial school, chapel and finally, in 1931, was converted to an apartment house.

Restoration began in 1944 and continued for more than ten years, sparked by the enthusiasm and gifts of Mrs. James Edward Latham, a native of New Bern, who had long cherished the hope of restoring Governor Tryon's palace to its onetime glory. The final restoration, done with meticulous research and the aid of the same Boston architects—Shaw and Hepburn—who had been in charge of the Williamsburg restoration, cost more than $3 million. It left the magnificent house and grounds as they might have been at the time of Governor Tryon's residence. In a special sense the restoration was extraordinary. It involved finding or making materials like those used in the original building. For its furnishings and decoration teams of buyers, aided by the full inventory Governor Tryon kept, combed England and Europe to acquire furniture, draperies, rugs, paintings, silverware and accessories. The extensive gardens, regarded as unique and marvelous in colonial days, may be so regarded today. Plants, flowers and shrubs in the ten sections of the garden are like those known to gardeners in the colonies before 1771, and range from an extensive kitchen garden to an unusual formal garden named for Mrs. Latham, whose benefactions made the restoration possible.

Since April, 1959, when the restoration was officially completed, visitors in increasing numbers have flocked through the restored palace and gardens, aided in their discovery by informed guides. Even those familiar with the superb Williamsburg restoration are likely to be astonished, for Tryon's Palace today is again one of the most beautiful buildings in America. Rooms and features of special interest include the massive and colorful arms of George III over the main entrance; the big, classically opulent council chamber, often converted to a ballroom, with its royal portraits and superb English furniture; the restored library with original editions of about five hundred books listed in Governor Tryon's inventory.

Most visitors find special interest in the big palace kitchen in the west wing, with its huge cooking fireplace, spit jack, crane and assortment of colonial utensils and cooking gear.

Tryon Palace, now owned and exhibited by the state of North Carolina, is easily reached. In the heart of New Bern, the visitor entrance is on George Street, between Eden and Metcalf streets, just a short distance east of US 17 and south of US 70. It is open to visitors every weekday except Monday, both morning and afternoon, and on Sunday afternoon.

IV

PATRIOTS AND FOUNDERS OF A NEW NATION

Settlement of the Eastern Seaboard, begun in the first years of the seventeenth century, continued for nearly a century and a half, steadily transforming a wilderness frontier into a cluster of prosperous colonies. By the middle of the eighteenth century early settlements had become thriving cities, forests had given way to productive fields, swift sailing vessels built in New England shipyards were carrying products of farms and plantations to ports all over the world. Mills and factories had been established, highways built.

As the colonies of England grew and prospered they became more and more self-sufficient, less and less responsive to laws and taxes established by the British parliament. They considered themselves no longer dependent satellites of England but copartners. Colonial troops helped England fight wars with France in Canada and the Indians of the western wilderness. Each of England's colonies in the New World had a royal governor but colonial assemblies were elected bodies where new concepts of government were beginning to flower.

In the last half of the eighteenth century they blossomed into open opposition to the repressive controls of a stubborn English monarch. Opposition, expressed in fervent speeches made in colonial assemblies, became rebellion and then war. It was a long, bitter, sometimes desperate war, but it united the colonies in a common purpose and produced a group of brilliant leaders and patriots. Colonial leaders meeting together in the former colonial capital of Philadelphia produced documents of association, first a Declaration of Independence and then a national Constitution, that turned thirteen former English colonies into a new nation, the United States of America.

The homes of some leaders who helped fight the war against the English and drafted the agreements by which the nation was formed are now cherished shrines. Most are also stately and beautiful dwellings. A selection of six of the homes of the founders of the new nation are described in the pages that follow. In three of them four Presidents of the United States lived. One was the home of a patriot famed for daring rides of warning during the Revolutionary War, and one, in a former colonial capital, was the home of a renowned teacher whose students included Presidents of the United States and signers of the Declaration of Independence and the Constitution.

Adams Houses, Quincy, Massachusetts

Certainly a most important group of family dwellings in America is a cluster of three houses in Quincy, Massachusetts, the historic seaport adjoining Boston on the south. In two of them, each a typical seventeenth-century saltbox cottage, Presidents of the United States were born. In one, John Adams, second President, was born in 1735. In the cottage next door his son, John Quincy Adams, sixth President, was born in 1767.

Just around the corner from these houses is a rambling colonial mansion where both John and John Quincy Adams lived for many years and where four generations of Adamses lived. In addition to producing two Presidents of the United States, the family claimed a long line of distinguished Americans: statesmen, soldiers, leaders of industry and writers. The two birthplace cottages given to the city of Quincy by Adams heirs in 1940 are now national historic landmarks. Following the death of Brooks Adams, the mansion was given to the United States government by the Adams heirs, becoming a national historic site in 1952.

Viewed together the three Adams houses in Quincy are an extraordinary demonstration of family continuity and life over nearly two hundred years. They were not an ordinary family, but one unmatched for achievement in America. The bright thread of Adams family history and the story of their homes begins with the birth of John Adams in 1735 in a cottage on Franklin Street in Quincy. The house where he was born is believed to have been built in 1681 and was acquired by John Adams' father, Deacon Adams, in 1720. It was a simple, almost primitive farmhouse, with two rooms downstairs and two on the upper floor. Later a lean-to was added at the rear. There was a central chimney with huge fireplace. Ceiling beams were hand hewn.

John Adams grew up in the house, living there until just before his marriage in 1764. Then he moved to the cottage next door, left to him by his father who died in 1761, believed to have been built about 1663. In the second house John Quincy Adams was born in 1767. From the second cottage John Adams embarked on his great public career as a distinguished leader of revolutionary activities during the last years of the colonial period. He was a member of the first and second Continental Congresses, one of the committee who helped draft the Declaration of Independence, one of the negotiators of peace with England, minister to England, and, in the new government, was Vice-President under General Washington, and was elected President of the United States in 1796.

The ancestral home of the illustrious Adams family of Massachusetts is a rambling colonial mansion at Quincy, Massachusetts, called Old House. *Photograph: Courtesy National Park Service.*

Great trees shade the wide lawns that surround Old House, where several generations of the Adams family lived for nearly 150 years. *Photograph: Courtesy National Park Service.*

Through this succession of great events John Adams' son grew to manhood, living most of the years of his youth in the house where he was born. There, for a number of years John Adams maintained his law office. Both the birthplace cottages are now maintained about as they were during the years members of the Adams family lived in them.

But as the resources and fame of the family grew the cottages proved inadequate. So in 1787, while serving as minister to England, John Adams acquired a larger, more elegant house around the corner. It became the Adams family home, lived in and extended over the years by four generations of Adamses.

The family mansion, which John Adams first called "Peacefield" but the family called the "Old House," had been built in 1731 by Major Leonard Vassall, a wealthy West Indian sugar planter. It was a handsome Georgian mansion typical of the period and not particularly large.

Over the years succeeding generations of Adamses managed to turn the historic house into a large, rambling mansion with various extensions and additions, starting with the first Adams owner, John Adams, who took possession of his new house on his return from England in 1788. While he was President he added a large gabled ell, with the famous and elegant long room downstairs and an upstairs study. In that room, sitting in a big wing chair in one corner, John Adams died on July 4, 1826, not long after his son became the sixth President of the United States. On that same day his old friend and close associate Thomas Jefferson also died. John Adams was ninety-one years old.

With the death of his father John Quincy Adams became master of the Old House, following a brilliant and varied career of public service, climaxed by his election to the Presidency. He had been minister to the Netherlands, minister to Prussia, minister to Russia, United States senator, member of the peace commission that signed the treaty ending the war of 1812, Secretary of State, and, after serving as President, became a member of Congress, dying from a heart attack on the floor of the House of Representatives in 1848, at the age of eighty-one. Twelve years before his death he had made his contribution to the Quincy mansion by adding a passage along the north side of the house connecting the two ells.

John Quincy Adams' son, Charles Francis Adams, was born in the family home in 1807. Following his graduation from Harvard he began, in the family tradition, a career of public service that included membership in Congress for two terms, minister to the Court of St. James's (both his father and grandfather had held the same post). Following his service abroad he returned to Quincy and the Old House to begin writing many volumes of family history. During that period he also made extensive changes and additions to the house. They included an extension of thirty feet to the kitchen ell for servant's quarters, the handsome two-story stone library overlooking the family garden just north of the house, and a stone stable and carriage house on the east edge of the estate. Charles Francis Adams died in 1886 at the age of seventy-nine.

John Adams, second President of the United States, was born in 1735 in this simple saltbox cottage built about 1681 at Quincy, Massachusetts. Photograph: Courtesy National Park Service.

The fourth Adams generation to call the Quincy mansion home were the four sons of Charles Francis Adams, John Quincy, Charles Francis, Jr., Henry and Brooks, who died in 1927, the last Adams to live in the family mansion.

Each member of the fourth Adams generation had a distinguished career. Collectively they included high-ranking military service during the Civil War, presidency of the Union Pacific Railway, membership on the board of governors of Harvard University, the authorship of important books and articles, as well as editorships of distinguished literary journals.

Of the four, only Brooks made any important changes in the structure of the house or its grounds. He added the walls and handsome gates opening on the front of the house from Adams Avenue, on the south.

Every generation of the family helped develop the present notable gardens and grounds. Extending over nearly five acres the grounds include extensive areas of lawn, many fine old trees, an eighteenth-century garden on the west side of the house, with plants and flowers that go back to a York Rose brought from England by Abigail Adams in 1788. Other elements of the grounds include a greenhouse, woodshed, duck pond and an orchard where some fruit trees are almost as old as the house itself.

Now beautifully maintained by the National Park Service, the Adams mansion and its grounds draw a steady stream of visitors. Most also visit the nearby birthplace cottages. Visitors find special fascination in the family mansion not because of its architectural character, which is not notable, or the beauty of its furnishings, but because of the intimate story it tells of the Adams family. The continuity of family life in the house is shown by its furnishings, as each new generation contributed something of itself. Adams' possessions seen in the house today, some intimate, some unique, include things collected from all over the world, particularly prized possessions of John, John Quincy and Charles Francis Adams, acquired on many diplomatic missions. Included are dozens of family portraits and portraits of important people with whom members of the family were closely associated, along with fine furniture of every period from classic examples of Georgian design to late Victorian pieces. Rooms of special interest include John Adams' study, with a desk used by four generations of the family, and, in a corner, the high-backed chair where John Adams died; the elegant long room, hung with family portraits, where three golden wedding anniversaries were celebrated; the dining room, with portraits of George and Martha Washington and furniture collected by each generation of the family. But the room that most visitors find of greatest interest is the splendid stone library built by Charles Francis Adams, a vast and remarkable room rising through two stories, its walls lined with thousands of books, family portraits and busts, its second-story balcony reached by a ladder.

The family mansion and the birthplace cottages are open daily, spring, summer and fall. The mansion is on Massachusetts Highway 135, not far from Massachusetts 3, with an entrance on Adams Street, about eight miles south of the center of Boston.

Paul Revere House, Boston, Massachusetts

A close friend and associate of John Adams during the troubled, dangerous days that led to the beginning of the Revolutionary War was the talented craftsman Paul Revere, leading silversmith of New England. Both men were members of the Sons of Liberty and both were deeply involved in the swirling events of the time, Adams as a political leader, Revere, who was a renowned horseman, as the official courier for the Massachusetts patriots.

Only surviving seventeenth-century house in downtown Boston, probably built about 1690, this cottage became famous as the home of Paul Revere, patriot, silversmith and celebrated horseman. *Photograph: Courtesy Massachusetts Department of Commerce.*

Paul Revere's home in Boston, which he acquired in 1770 and lived in for nearly thirty years, was a frame house near the crest of a hill in north Boston. The house is important for several reasons: architecturally as a fine example of an urban house of the seventeenth century, downtown Boston's only surviving seventeenth-century dwelling; historically as the home of an outstanding patriot and leader of the revolutionary period, and because during the beginning of the Revolutionary War it was involved in stirring and dramatic events.

The house today, carefully restored to its seventeenth-century appearance, is at 19 North Square, in what is now a crowded Italian district. In Paul Revere's day it was on the edge of a relatively new district of scattered houses with large gardens. It was then and is still within sight of historic Old North Church, the spire of which exhibited on the night of April 18, 1775, two lighted lanterns as a signal to patriots in Charlestown that the British were headed for Lexington and Concord by boat. Paul Revere had arranged the signal and when the lanterns were hung slipped out of the back door of the house on the first stage of what would become within a few hours the most famous and fateful gallop in history. He could not use the front door since the whole square in front of his house was crowded with British redcoats waiting to start their journey to Lexington.

About two months later members of Paul Revere's family watched British marines trundle naval cannon to the crest of Copp's Hill to bombard Charlestown and the American patriots' lines entrenched on Bunker hill. Over a period of several hours the roar of the cannon shook the Revere house.

Paul Revere, soon deeply involved in the military action of the war, did not return to his house in north Boston until the next year, when, after General Washington drove the British from Boston, he took charge of the fort on Castle Island, and began to devote his energy and talents to supplying American troops with munitions and equipment. He lived in the north Boston house until 1800.

The story of the Paul Revere house began in 1676, soon after the great fire of the previous year had destroyed most of the wooden buildings of Boston. The builder was John Jeffs, who erected a characteristically medieval 17th-century house of two and a half stories. When Paul Revere moved in about a hundred years later it had grown to three full stories and was steep-roofed, with an extended second floor. Inside there is a large room, or hall, spanned by massive beams, two big fireplaces, three other rooms and an attic. Windows are small, with diamond-shaped panes. At the rear on the ground floor is a kitchen, with brick ovens and ancient utensils. It was from the back door of the kitchen that Paul Revere left to begin his ride.

During the nineteenth century, after Paul Revere's death in 1819, the old house in north Boston degenerated into a tenement and store, and was greatly modified over the years. Rescued in 1908 by the Paul Revere Memorial Association, it was carefully restored, and today is seen by visitors as it probably looked during the late seventeenth and early eighteenth centuries, furnished with pieces typical of the period (not much of it Revere's). Ornaments and souvenirs exhibited in the house include examples of Revere's silverwork, some of his etchings and manuscripts.

Most people who visit the old house continue up the hill to Paul Revere Plaza, where there is a handsome statue of the patriot mounted on a galloping steed. Then they go on to the Old North Church, where they can see one of the two lanterns that hung in the tower. Just north of the church is an old burying ground of great charm, where British cannons once stood to bombard Charlestown, with the graves of many who were Paul Revere's friends and neighbors. At the river's edge below the hill Paul Revere retrieved a previously hidden boat to row across the river and begin galloping toward Lexington and into fame.

In 1770, Thomas Jefferson began to build Monticello. The superb thirty-five-room mansion was his home for the rest of a long life.
Photograph: Courtesy Virginia State Travel Service.

Monticello, Thomas Jefferson Home, Charlottesville, Virginia

No home in the country more clearly reflects the character and special genius of its owner than does the hilltop mansion, Monticello, Thomas Jefferson built southeast of Charlottesville, Virginia.

Jefferson, who in time would become author of the Declaration of Independence, governor of Virginia, minister to France, Secretary of State and third President of the United States, was born in 1743 on a farm near the village of Shadwell, Virginia, in the Blue Ridge foothills and on the western frontier of Colonial Virginia. The region would be his home for the rest of

Seen between entrance gates,
Jefferson's splendid mansion
presents an immaculate façade
to an equally immaculate
snow-covered lawn.
*Photograph: Courtesy
Virginia State Travel Service.*

his life. The farm of his birth was part of a grant of one thousand acres received by Jefferson's father in 1735. It passed to Thomas, on his father's death twenty-two years later.

Jefferson attended Virginia's famed William and Mary College where he studied law under the gifted scholar and barrister George Wythe and was admitted to the bar in 1767. Then he returned to the mountain estate near Charlottesville, left him by his father. On Jefferson's land was a small forested mountain rising to 857 feet above sea level. In 1768 Jefferson decided to make it the site for a home which he would call "Monticello," Italian for "little mountain." He cleared access trails to the crest of his mountain and leveled an area there. In 1770 he began building his house from meticulous plans that reflected his special talent as an architect. It would be 1809 before the unique and splendid house was finally completed. But over the years it was Jefferson's only home, his beloved Monticello.

Jefferson planned and supervised virtually everything himself, employing skills of artisan slaves for the actual building. Material for the building—stone, brick, lumber, even nails—came from the estate, fashioned on the site to fit the remarkable plans Jefferson drew. In 1772 the first unit of the mansion was completed, a templelike pavilion that became known as the honeymoon cottage. To it Jefferson brought his bride, Martha Wayles Skelton, coming to the new home on horseback, during a blizzard. Thereafter Monticello grew with the years, with Jefferson supervising the growth. The result that visitors see today, maintained about as it was during the last years of Jefferson's life, is one of the most remarkable and handsome dwellings in America, a near perfect example of American Classic Revival, with emphasis on Roman elements.

In some ways Monticello is remarkable, in several ways unique. Few houses command a more spectacular setting, a mountain crest with a far view in all directions. Jefferson took full advantage of it, with clearings cut through the trees to permit fine vistas, putting his house in the center of twelve acres of lawn. The mansion itself is perfectly symmetrical in design, with long, L-shaped balustraded terraces extending from the north and south, a pavilion of classic design at the end of each, the main house at the bottom and center of a U, overlooking a rolling lawn of several acres. The terraces served a special purpose, to roof, protect and conceal small outbuildings such as laundry, smokehouse, kitchen, dairy, stable, weaving room, wine room and beer cellar. The profile of the terraces is low, in no way obstructing the appearance of the main dwelling, which brings the attention of all visitors to a sharp focus. The house, almost majestically beautiful, contains thirty-five rooms, including twelve in the basement. Matching, white-columned Roman porticos extend from the east and west. Rising above them, at the intersection of converging roof lines, is the dominating feature of the house, a low octagonal dome.

Impressive as the outside of the house is, the real excitement of Monticello for most visitors is the interior. For variety and surprise no other house anywhere can match it. It is distinguished by beauty of woodwork and dozens of examples of Jefferson's extraordinary inventive genius and wide-

Adjoining dining rooms at Monticello were used to entertain visitors to the Jeffersons' hilltop mansion.
Photograph: Courtesy Virginia State Travel Service.
▷

Some fascinating details are grouped over the main entrance door: a huge clock of special design, and matching elk horns.
Photograph: Courtesy Virginia State Travel Service.

ranging interests. In addition the house is filled with mementos and souvenirs of Jefferson's public service, from exquisite examples of French china, to elk and moose horns on either side of the door of the main entrance that were sent to Jefferson in 1804 by Lewis and Clark. The antlers frame the most spectacular of Jefferson's many inventions scattered through the house: a huge seven-day clock that tells the day of the week by cannon balls descending against a scale. Other Jeffersonian gadgets include dumbwaiters, revolving doors, disappearing beds, unusual lighting and ventilating arrangements, a duplicate writing machine, folding doors, storm windows.

The most impressive room is the ballroom or dome room, under the central dome, but the one visitors find most interesting is Jefferson's study and bedroom, with a specially designed bed in between the rooms so that, whatever his mood, Jefferson could get out of bed on the side that served it. In the study is Jefferson's favorite writing device, a combination swivel chair and chaise longue in front of a revolving-top writing table.

A distinctive feature of the mansion is the absence of a traditional main stairway. Instead, Jefferson, in the interest of economy of space, privacy and better ventilation, built very narrow winding stairways, extending from the basement to the second floors and concealed them by doors. No longer in the house is Jefferson's huge library that once filled a room off his study. The original library books, about sixty-five hundred volumes, were sold to the government as the nucleus of a new Library of Congress in Washington, after the original Library of Congress burned.

The extensive gardens of the Monticello estate, neglected for many years, have been meticulously restored since 1940 and reflect Jefferson's high interest in horticulture and botany. Restoration was aided by detailed descriptions of the original garden found in Jefferson's notebooks, including lists of plants for each bed, with instructions for tending them. They include some imported from France. A feature of the lawn-garden area, also restored, is a large fish pond, which in Jefferson's day was kept well stocked with fish caught in nearby streams.

Fish from Jefferson's own pond were often served during dinners at which Jefferson entertained a stream of visitors. During his last years at Monticello the mansion was a mecca for distinguished travelers, so that it was not uncommon for him to receive and entertain as many as forty or fifty guests a day. Jefferson's open-handed hospitality so impoverished him that during the final years of his life his once substantial resources were almost completely dissipated.

Jefferson died on July 4, 1826, on the fiftieth anniversary of the signing of the Declaration of Independence. He was eighty-three years old. By a quirk of history one of his old friends and associates, John Adams, second President of the United States, died on the same day. Jefferson was buried in a private burial ground, part of the Monticello estate, not far from the mansion. Though the mansion itself passed through various ownerships, title to the burial plot has never left the control of Jefferson descendants, whose members have a right to burial there.

Following Jefferson's death evil days beset the splendid Monticello estate. In 1831 it was sold by Jefferson's only surviving child, Mrs. Martha Jefferson Randolph, together with 552 acres for about a tenth of its actual worth. The purchaser, a Mr. Barkley, disliked Jefferson and managed to destroy most of the gardens. The estate, or at least part of it was rescued briefly by Commodore Uriah Levy, who admired Jefferson and hoped to restore the house. But these hopes were deferred for many years, while the house, occupied by tenants, faced progressive ruin. Then after the end of the Civil War gradual restoration began under the direction of the Levy family, who in 1923 sold the estate and about 650 acres to the Thomas Jefferson Memorial Foundation for $500,000.

Since then restoration and maintenance have been under the direction of the foundation, along with the collection and restoration of hundreds of things that Jefferson owned. The near-perfect result, the full splendor of Monticello as it existed at the peak of its fame as Jefferson's home, is what visitors see today.

Monticello is easily reached. It is three miles southeast of downtown Charlottesville on Virginia Highway 53, the route clearly indicated by highway signs. The house and gardens are open daily March through October from 8 A.M. to 5 P.M., the rest of the year until 4:30 P.M.

Mount Vernon, George Washington Home, Virginia

The most famous farmhouse in the nation is a white-pillared colonial mansion overlooking the Potomac River about fifteen miles south of Washington, D.C. Called Mount Vernon, it was named for a British admiral, and for nearly fifty years was the plantation home of George Washington. Today, superbly restored and maintained, it is visited by more people than any private dwelling in the country. They see not only the beautiful colonial mansion full of General Washington's possessions, but the best example in America of a complete colonial plantation maintained as it was at the height of its productivity.

The story of Mount Vernon began in 1674 when John Washington acquired a tract of five thousand acres, part of a royal grant made to Lord Culpepper. In 1735 his grandson, Augustine, built a small house on the site,

▷
Most familiar façade of any
private dwelling in the
country is the white-pillared
porch of Mount Vernon,
home of George Washington.
*Photograph: Courtesy
Virginia State Travel Service.*

nucleus of the present mansion, at the crest of a bluff above the Potomac. He moved his family there from a plantation called Wakefield (see page 75), where George Washington had been born in 1732. Augustine's new home was a simple house of one and a half stories, little more than a cottage, in no way resembling the gracious mansion that stands there now. In 1739 a fire that destroyed most of the house sent the family to Fredericksburg. The land was given to Lawrence, Augustine's oldest son and older half-brother of George. In 1743 Lawrence rebuilt the destroyed house, named it Mount Vernon in honor of Admiral Vernon under whom he had served in the West Indies. When Lawrence died in 1752, George Washington became the proprietor of Mount Vernon. It was to be his home for the rest of his life.

In 1759 Washington brought his bride, Martha Dandridge Custis, a well-to-do widow with two children, to Mount Vernon. Over the years, acting as his own architect, Washington changed the house in many ways, adding an additional story, extending it to the north and south. He also extended and developed his lands, from an original 2,126 acres to about eight thousand, divided into five farms, one of the finest and most profitable plantation estates in the country. The Mount Vernon mansion was the estate office, center of a cluster of workshops and mills, including a gristmill and distillery. Washington's dock on the Potomac was regularly visited by commercial craft that loaded farm produce for distribution and sale or brought to the estate many things Washington bought abroad. Among the estate staff of several hundred, most of them slaves, were carpenters, blacksmiths, weavers, bricklayers and other skilled craftsmen. At a time when most Americans were farmers, Washington was one of the wealthiest. Vivid evidence of that wealth can be seen at Mount Vernon today in the superbly planned mansion with its cluster of outbuildings and gardens, all neatly arranged in a symmetrical pattern, joined by graceful arcades.

When Washington died in 1799 he was buried, as he had wished, on the estate grounds. In 1802 Martha Washington died and was buried beside her husband. For the next fifty years heirs of Washington tried, without much success, to maintain the property. Finally in 1850, John A. Washington, Jr., last private owner, without funds to maintain the estate, tried without success to sell it either to the state of Virginia or to the federal government.

Then in 1856 a remarkable woman, Ann Pamela Cunningham of South Carolina, decided that Mount Vernon should be a national shrine. She organized the Mount Vernon Ladies Association, which raised $200,000, and bought the estate along with two hundred surrounding acres. The association, which still owns and exhibits the property, has diligent members in thirty states dedicated to the single purpose of making Mount Vernon what it was at the height of the period of Washington's ownership. It has superbly restored the house and the grounds that surround it, now about five hundred acres, the approximate area of the original mansion house farm. Year after year by purchase, donation, indefinite loan and bequests, many of the furnishings that were at Mount Vernon during Washington's life have been reassembled.

Many American bedrooms are faithful copies of this handsome master bedroom at Mount Vernon, with its mahogany posterbed and quilted white counterpane. *Photograph: Courtesy Virginia State Travel Service.*

As a national shrine Mount Vernon is unique and inspiring, an intimate reflection of the life and character of one of the greatest Americans. The mansion itself, gleaming white, with a red roof and cupola, walls that resemble stone, but are actually wooden slabs carved to look like stone, is surrounded by the outbuildings that show the plantation's working character, coach house, spinning house, slave quarters where about sixty of the two hundred slaves Washington owned lived. The mansion itself is a fine example of colonial architecture. Its familiar white-columned porch, running along the entire length of the east side overlooking the Potomac, has probably been adapted to more fine houses than any other single architectural detail. The beautifully maintained rooms of the mansion are full of the things Washington used, had made or imported for his wife and family. They range from the simplest candle snuffer to a handsome harpsichord brought from England at a cost of one thousand pounds for his step-granddaughter, Nellie Custis. There are many portraits, including some famous ones by Charles Wilson Peale and Gilbert Stuart. There are many things that were presented to Washington over the years. The most celebrated is probably the key to the Bastille of France given to Washington by General Lafayette. Many visitors regard Washington's study as the most interesting room. It is filled with books, thousands of letters, and has Washington's voluminous diary.

Though the mansion itself is the central exhibit, visitors find fascination in the beautifully kept gardens and grounds maintained as Washington designed and planted them, with many of the plants descendants of those that grew in Washington's day. Garden experts regard the grounds as some of the finest in the East.

There is, in addition to restored buildings and some faithful copies of others that have disappeared, one new building (and, of course, service buildings at the entrance gate). It is a museum and administration building where hundreds of relics relating to Washington that could not be shown in the mansion itself are exhibited. Its most renowned exhibit is the original clay model of the familiar bust of Washington, modeled from life at Mount Vernon in 1785 by the French sculptor Houdon, copied on postage stamps and coins of the country.

A poignant pilgrimage for most visitors is a short walk down a sloping lawn from one side of the mansion to a brick crypt where George and Martha Washington are buried.

Not now part of the Mount Vernon estate proper, although once on the original mansion house farm, is the Mount Vernon gristmill, authentically restored, once a busy center for a blacksmith shop, cooper shop and distillery. Washington claimed that the mill's flour and whisky were the equal in quality to any in Virginia. The mill is three miles from Mount Vernon on Virginia Highway 235, just east of Richmond Road US 1.

Mount Vernon is open every day after 9 A.M., with entrance gates closed at 5 P.M., spring, summer and fall; at 4 P.M. during winter months. There are two highway routes to the mansion and grounds: US 1, linking

The portrait of an English queen is only one of the many elegant details in the richly appointed dining room of George Washington's plantation home. *Photograph: Courtesy Virginia State Travel Service.*

Washington with Richmond, Virginia, and the Mount Vernon Memorial Highway, along the west shore of the Potomac River. Both are linked to the Capitol Beltway, Interstate 495.

George Wythe House, Williamsburg, Virginia

Few communities can claim more historic houses than the extraordinary little city of Colonial Williamsburg, Virginia. They range from the splendid Governors Palace, official residence of royal governors of the colony of Virginia, to small, charming colonial cottages. All were part of the busy life of Colonial Williamsburg when that community was a gem among the British capital cities in the New World.

Among historic Williamsburg houses one in particular is unique. It is the George Wythe House, a solid brick mansion on the west side of the Palace Green, named for its owner, George Wythe, who lived there from the time of his marriage about 1754 until he was murdered by a greedy grandnephew in 1806. During the period of his residence in Williamsburg George Wythe became one of the most influential Americans of his era, whose life and work as a colonial patriot, lawyer and teacher helped shape the careers of many Americans.

But the Wythe House is also important architecturally, as a near-perfect example of domestic colonial design of the Georgian period. Now one of the outstanding restorations of Colonial Williamsburg, it gives a vivid, authentic glimpse of how well-to-do colonial leaders lived and worked when Williamsburg was an influential colonial capital.

Wythe (pronounced to rhyme with Smith) was a typical product of plantation society in Virginia in an era when plantations were prosperous and extensive and their owners cultured members of their communities. Wythe's father was a successful planter in Elizabeth City in a Tidewater region not far from Williamsburg. Born in 1726 George Wythe entered William and Mary College while still in his teens. He read widely in the classics and in time became the foremost classical scholar of Virginia. But his first love was law. Only twenty years old when he was admitted to the bar, he practiced law in Spotsylvania for a few years, returning to Williamsburg about 1754. It was his home thereafter.

At about the time he returned to Williamsburg Wythe married Elizabeth Taliaferro, daughter of Colonel Richard Taliaferro who was a gifted amateur architect. The colonel used his talents to design and build a modest mansion for his daughter and new son-in-law. Wythe was soon embarked on a long dual career of public service and teaching, filling a succession of posts: burgess, Clerk of the House, Speaker of the House of Delegates, a judge of Virginia's High Court of Chancery. His name appears first among Virginia's signers of the Declaration of Independence.

But though his public career was extensive and important Wythe is best remembered as a brilliant teacher of law. His students included Thomas Jefferson and John Marshall, who became a celebrated Chief Justice of the

A near-perfect example of colonial domestic design: the George Wythe House at Colonial Williamsburg as seen from the rear gardens. *Photograph: Courtesy Colonial Williamsburg.*

Supreme Court. In 1779 Wythe was appointed to the newly established chair of law at William and Mary College, and so became the first professor of law in an American college.

Wythe was a mild-mannered, soft-spoken man of great erudition with a special gift of friendship. The relation between him and many of his students was one of cordial intimacy. They visited him at his home beside the Palace Green, and often worked there. In the house today visitors see a student's room set with the accessories of study. Of Wythe, Jefferson wrote: "He was my faithful and beloved Mentor in youth, and my most affectionate friend through life." When Jefferson was a leader of colonial affairs he and his family often visited the Wythe house.

George Wythe, distinguished
scholar and statesman, lived
for many many years in this
typical eighteenth-century
townhouse in Colonial
Williamsburg. *Photograph:
Courtesy Colonial
Williamsburg.*

▷

In the students' room of the
George Wythe House in
Colonial Williamsburg, the
young men whom Wythe
taught, including Thomas
Jefferson, often studied. The
room's accessories included
scientific apparatus they used.
*Photograph: Courtesy
Colonial Williamsburg.*

But Wythe's brilliant career ended in sordid tragedy. He was poisoned by arsenic added to strawberries, though the crime was not proven because Virginia law would not accept testimony of a slave who saw it done. The murderer almost certainly was Wythe's grandnephew, George Sweeney, grandson of Wythe's only sister. Deeply and dangerously in debt through excessive gambling Sweeney hoped to be the principal beneficiary of his uncle. Ironically he failed. Though dying in agony of the poison Wythe managed to change his will, leaving his grandnephew nothing.

Thanks to skillful restoration, the Wythe house today appears to visitors about as it was when it was a center of important events. It was the headquarters of Washington before the siege of Yorktown, and for Rochambeau after the surrender of Cornwallis at Yorktown. Following Wythe's death it passed through the hands of several owners, and was acquired by Colonial Williamsburg in 1938, when careful restoration of the house and grounds was completed.

The mansion, almost classic in design, is simple but spacious and completely symmetrical, with all elements in perfect balance. Built of brick, laid in a pattern and with skill characteristic of late seventeenth-century brick masons, it is solid and square, rising two stories under a hip-roof, with the roof line broken by massive chimneys on either side, so placed to permit a fireplace in each of the eight rooms of the house, four on each floor.

Since no inventory of the furnishings of the house has been discovered and few of Wythe's own possessions found, the house has been refurnished with the guidance of inventories of similar houses owned by men whose wealth and background approximated those of Wythe. Though a typical townhouse, the grounds are unusually extensive, forming a plantation layout in miniature. There is a large kitchen garden adjoining a smokehouse and henhouse. Adjoining the kitchen garden is a herb garden. The rear façade of the house commands an extensive lawn, set with boxwood, typical of the evergreen gardens of Williamsburg. All the garden and associated area has been restored with care, and probably resembles the garden where George Wythe sat on summer evenings discussing law, literature and politics with his students and friends.

The house is open to visitors to Williamsburg on alternate days as one of the featured exhibits of Colonial Williamsburg.

Characteristic of many houses of the period, the George Wythe House in Colonial Williamsburg had a central hall opening front and back, and an angled, banistered stairway leading to upper rooms. *Photograph: Courtesy Colonial Williamsburg.*

American-built furniture of the late
eighteenth century graced the Wythe
House dining room of Colonial Williamsburg. The portrait is of St. George Tucker,
who succeeded Wythe as professor of law
at William and Mary College. *Photograph:
Courtesy Colonial Williamsburg.*

V

PIONEERS AND FRONTIER DWELLERS

Before the end of the Revolutionary War a trickle of settlers began trudging west through the passes of the Alleghenies seeking new homes in the wide western wilderness. Trappers and Indian fighters had told of its character: great rivers, vast forests, fertile land. But with the end of the war the trickle became a steady stream of hopeful migrants moving with ox-drawn wagons, and on keelboats and rafts down the broad rivers. Thousands chopped clearings in the forest and built primitive cabins of logs. In some of the cabins children were born who in time became such famous Americans that the cabins are now preserved as shrines.

As the years went on, and the United States acquired vast new lands west of the Mississippi River from France and later from Mexico, streams of immigrants moved steadily westward, often in great caravans of covered wagons that were called prairie schooners. They trekked over the plains and prairies and scaled the craggy ramparts of the western mountains to make the far limit of their lands the Pacific Ocean. The pioneering settlement of the central valley, the plains and prairies beyond, the conquering of the western mountains and settlement of the Pacific slope continued beyond the middle of the nineteenth century. It was marked by events: the purchase of vast new lands from France, two wars with England and Mexico and the discovery of gold in California.

From the long period of western settlement pioneers and leaders emerged who became renowned Americans: soldiers, Indian fighters, political leaders. Some of the homes where they were born or lived have become shrines and memorials. Three of the men became Presidents of the United States, one was a renowned Indian scout. One planned and led the greatest of all western migrations that resulted in the settlement of Utah by the Mormon people. One helped trigger the discovery of California gold, one was a famous teacher and author, and one, born in a log cabin as a Negro slave, became a renowned leader of his people. The stories of their lives as pioneers and frontier dwellers and their homes on the frontiers of the West are told in pages that follow.

Beehive House, Brigham Young Home, Salt Lake City, Utah

The most remarkable pioneer of the westward migration was the resolute leader of the Mormon people, Brigham Young. Born in a log cabin on a Vermont farm in 1801, he had almost no formal schooling, was taught to read by his mother. But when he was fourteen years old his mother died and Brigham became an apprentice in carpentry and cabinet-making.

By the time he was thirty he was a skilled craftsman making his living at carpentry in the village of Mendon, New York, living in a house that he had built himself for his wife and two daughters. Then, by chance, he read the Book of Mormon, and soon decided to join the Church of Jesus Christ of the Latter Day Saints.

He soon became a missionary and dedicated his life to his church. From the church headquarters in Kirtland, Ohio, he was sent to Canada by the young church leader Prophet Joseph Smith; later he led a caravan of converts to Kirtland from New York. He helped Prophet Smith plan and build the remarkable Mormon city of Nauvoo, Illinois. There in 1844 mounting resentment against the Mormon people flared into violence, and led to the death of Prophet Smith at the hands of a mob.

Brigham Young became Smith's successor, acknowledged leader of the Mormon people, who during the winter of 1846 deserted their great but beleaguered city of Nauvoo. Leaving it and its splendid temple to pillaging mobs, they headed west over a wilderness of prairie and plain, in one of the most extraordinary migrations of history.

About fifteen thousand Mormons left Nauvoo, with their possessions loaded in covered wagons. The main body camped for the winter near Council Bluffs, Iowa, but Brigham Young headed an advance wagon train of several thousand over the frozen wastes of the high plains. He was determined to find a place beyond the mountains of the West, where, isolated from the rest of the world, his people could live in peace.

The incredible journey, marked by hardship and disaster, ended in the hot summer of 1847. After toiling up the eastern slopes of the Rocky Mountains the wagon train reached the crest of a pass and began a slow descent over craggy slopes, through canyons and forests. Then, almost suddenly, Brigham Young and his followers emerged from a canyon to look west over dry foothills to a scene of desolation. The foothills tumbled below the pass merged into a rolling waste of desert. In the distance was the shimmer of water, which would become known as Great Salt Lake. Beyond alkali flats, rising through the summer heat were crests of distant mountains. Young and his followers were looking across what geologists call the Great Basin, once the bed of a huge prehistoric lake. Taking in the prospect from the pass Brigham Young, it is claimed, said: "This is the place." It must have taken remarkable imagination to see in the arid wilderness anything that might be converted into a future home for the Mormon people.

But it *was* "the place," for the Mormon pioneers settled there to establish what would become Salt Lake City. By a combination of ingenuity and perseverance they began to transform the dry foothill land into homesites and farms, damming the mountain streams and ditching the slopes to provide water for gardens and farms in the first modern irrigation system in the country.

The first few years were bitterly hard. Vast swarms of crickets devoured precious ripening grain. Heavy frosts destroyed crops. There was widespread disease and hunger. Only sharing everything prevented complete disaster. But the settlement survived and grew, as more and more Mormon pioneers arrived from the East.

Seven years after the first group of Mormons reached the Great Basin, when Salt Lake City, though laid out with wide streets befitting a modern metropolis, was still a raw pioneer settlement of a few thousand people, Brigham Young planned and directed the construction of the Beehive House. At the same time he directed the building of a great temple to stand a short distance west of Beehive House. The temple would take forty years to complete. But Beehive House, his family home and official residence, was soon completed.

There are several remarkable things about Beehive House, today a Salt Lake City landmark that fascinates thousands of visitors. Perhaps the most remarkable is that a house of its character could be built at all at that time and in that place. During the settlement of the western frontier few large houses of architectural grace and sophistication of design could be built, since most pioneer settlers of the period lacked the knowledge of design and building skills that were needed. And the land itself seldom provided the materials necessary for construction.

Beehive House was an exception. Mormon pioneers were not ordinary frontier dwellers. Among them were men of varied skills, architects and craftsmen of many kinds. Brigham Young himself was such a specialist. To help him Young enlisted the aid of a gifted architect, Truman O. Angell, who also designed the extraordinary many-spired Salt Lake City Temple. The style Young and Angell selected for the Beehive House was a happy choice: Greek revival, then widely popular throughout New England and part of the Middle West.

The land itself provided the material: stone and adobe for walls, timbers cut from forests to the east for frame and woodwork. A corps of craftsmen skilled in wood and metal-working cut and shaped materials. The result was a house of dignity and charm.

When completed the Beehive House was a rectangular two-story house and attic. Walls were adobe. Slender square columns, typical of the Greek Revival style, permitted a ground floor porch on the south and east sides and supported a railed balcony on the second floor. Four chimneys thrust from a graceful roof, framing a high terrace or "widow's walk" within a wooden railing (now wrought iron), an anachronistic detail suggesting the

coast of seafaring New England where waiting women might first see the sails of returning ships. From the center of the high terrace a wooden cupola supported a huge golden beehive, traditional Mormon symbol of industry. Exteriors of the thick adobe walls were plastered and painted a straw yellow color. All exterior woodwork was white. Several years after its completion Young had a nine-foot-high rough stone wall built around the shallow plot where the house stood. It served a dual purpose: as a barrier to unwelcome intruders and a make-work project for unemployed stone-masons.

The interior of the house involved a most successful combination of colonial and New England styles with imaginative designs of frontier crafts-men. Much of the woodwork was colonial, some walls handsomely paneled in wood. Decorative details echoed Mormon symbols, including the busy bee. Throughout the house imagination and mechanical ingenuity practiced by Brigham Young's Yankee craftsmen provided unusual conveniences, that today delight and astonish visitors to the house.

For thirty-three years the Beehive House was Brigham Young's home. There his children grew up and received part of their education in a special schoolroom. There Young maintained his personal office. The house was also the official Mormon mansion where leaders of the Church met, and where Brigham Young entertained important visitors to Salt Lake City. They included President Ulysses S. Grant, Dom Pedro, Emperor of Brazil, General William T. Sherman, Ralph Waldo Emerson, Mark Twain, Jay Gould, Horace Greeley and the celebrated midget Tom Thumb and his tiny wife.

It was Brigham Young's home and headquarters until his death in 1877. It was a big house for its day, and a comfortable one; but it was not big enough for Young's growing family. Wives and children overflowed the Beehive House, and Young soon built the Lion House just west of the Bee-hive House.

The interior furnishings of Victorian and other styles reflect the heri-tage of the owner and his associates. Much of the furniture was carried west in covered wagons over a period of several decades. Some were designed and built by Young himself during the period of his cabinetmaking in New England. Some pieces were made in Salt Lake City by pioneer craftsmen copying furniture they remembered.

During the years of Young's life in Beehive House Salt Lake City grew to be the center of Mormon life. Eight years before Young's death in 1877, the first transcontinental railway was completed at Promontory, Utah, a few miles northwest of Salt Lake City, and the isolation which Brigham Young sought when he led the Mormon pioneers into the wilderness was gone forever.

After Brigham Young's death two major alterations were made in the Beehive House. A son of Brigham Young, who bought the house in 1888, rebuilt the rear section into a three-story wing, and extensively remodeled the downstairs dining room. A few years later the Church bought the his-

Beehive House, in the heart of Salt Lake City, was the home of Mormon leader Brigham Young and his family for many years. *Photograph: Courtesy Church Information Service, Church of Jesus Christ of Latter Day Saints.*

117

A fascinating room is Brigham
Young's bedroom, full of fine
Victorian furniture and
intimate personal relics of
Brigham Young's life.
*Photograph: Courtesy Church
Information Service, Church
of Jesus Christ of Latter Day
Saints.*

The cluttered kitchen vividly
suggests the living habits of
a big family during the
Victorian era. *Photograph:
Courtesy Church Information
Service, Church of Jesus
Christ of Latter Day Saints.*

toric house to use as the official residence for its presidents. However, only two ever lived there. For a period the house was empty, then it was re-modeled again to use as a residence for young women who came to the city to work or go to school.

Finally, in 1959, the Church decided to restore the house to its original condition. The job of restoration, carried out with the aid of old plans and manuscripts, was done with skill and taste, including restoration of original schemes of decoration and furnishings. Much of Brigham Young's original furniture was located, refinished and restored to the house, with other pieces typical of the period found and placed in the house. Intimate accessories used by the Young family were also located and restored.

Today the historic old house, just a short walk east of Temple Square, draws thousands of visitors each year. Carefully trained guides, familiar with the character and meaning of everything in the house, lead groups from room to room. Visitors see an almost perfect example of an upper-class Victorian home of the last decade of the nineteenth century as it was lived in by a large and devoted family. Rooms of special interest include Brigham Young's own room, filled with his things; schoolroom and playroom; a classically elegant main dining room; and the ornate Long Hall where notables were entertained. Most visitors find special fascination in the kitchen and storeroom, where bins, barrels and boxes again store produce typical of that produced on the Brigham Young farm, and where ingenious pioneer gadgets such as a mechanical apple peeler and a castiron pump still work.

Grouseland, William Henry Harrison Home, Vincennes, Indiana

Toward the end of the eighteenth century the vast, splendid forest wilderness north of the Ohio River and east of the Wabash River was beginning to be settled. The pattern of settlement was usually the same. A pioneer family would enter the forest from the Ohio River, hack out a clearing, build a primitive log cabin, establish a corn patch and begin to live off the land. Many clearings in time became villages, then towns. Some grew to cities. The forest in time disappeared.

There was little difference between one forest clearing and others in most of the huge region then called the Northwest Territory, with one exception—Vincennes on the Wabash River.

Vincennes was a permanent community, a French one. A fur trading post had been established there as early as 1702, and a few years later a church was built which became a cathedral. About 1730 a fort was built and the thriving village, center of trade and culture for a wide area, was named Vincennes, for the French officer who commanded it. Vincennes had paved streets lined with whitewashed log houses that were behind picket fences. There were orchards and gardens and a growing number of modest industries.

An important thing about Vincennes was its strategic location on the wide channel of the Wabash River, linking Vincennes to New Orleans to the south and to the wilderness empire of France to the north. At Vincennes another route of wilderness travel met and crossed the river, a buffalo trail angling northwest from the Ohio River into Illinois. The buffalo had all been driven away or killed by 1800 but the trail was still there. So Vincennes, the growing French town, was a strategic target for conquest, first by the English during the French and Indian War, then by the wilderness fighters from the new American nation, which took Vincennes away from the British in one of the most daring military adventures of American history.

Thus it is not surprising that in 1800 when Congress decided to create a territory from the wilderness they had wrested from the British, they selected Vincennes as territorial capital. The vast region would in time become the states of Wisconsin, Indiana, Illinois, Michigan and part of what would be Minnesota.

President Adams appointed a twenty-seven-year-old Virginian, William Henry Harrison, as governor of the new territory. Born at Berkeley Plantation on the James River in Virginia, young Harrison was a Virginia aristocrat, member of a celebrated family. In time he would become a military hero and the ninth President of the United States, helped in both by his achievements as governor of the Indiana territory.

Harrison reached Vincennes in January, 1801, traveling over the old buffalo trail. The finest and newest house in Vincennes was offered for his use. It had just been built by the Sardinian pioneer and fur trader Francis Vigo, leading citizen of Vincennes. But Governor Harrison decided that the needs of his family and the prestige of his office required a finer dwelling. So he built one, patterning it after a Virginia plantation mansion, although the governor's new home was neither large nor impressive. But for the frontier of Vincennes it was splendid, finer and more elegant than any other dwelling in the region. The site was a three-hundred-acre tract along the Wabash River, north of the village of Vincennes, and included a fine grove of walnut trees.

First brick house in Vincennes, the official home of the governor had a handsome pillared two-story porch facing the river. The house was two stories high with a basement and attic, and twenty-six rooms in the main or "great house" with a smaller dependency in the rear later linked to the larger house by a covered corridor on the ground floor and an enclosed corridor on the second floor. There were ten fireplaces with richly carved mantels. All the elements and material for the new house came from local sources, except the doors, stairways, windows and the fireplace mantels, which the governor arranged to bring west from Virginia. Stone for the foundations came from a Kentucky quarry; 200,000 bricks were made from clay found on a neighboring farm. The heavy timbers for the house were hewn from forest trees cut nearby and the hand-forged nails were made by Vincennes blacksmiths.

When completed in 1804 the governor's big new mansion was a marvel to the people of Vincennes and to the stream of visitors who came to call,

Grouseland, completed in 1804 as the
official residence of Governor William
Harrison of the Northwest Territory, was
the finest house on the wilderness frontier.
It resembled the plantation mansions of
Harrison's Tidewater Virginia.
Photograph: Courtesy Gary Long, W. M.
Cline Company, Vigo County Chapter
Daughters of the American Revolution.

A handsome feature of
Grouseland is the graceful
colonial stairway at the end
of the wide central hall.
Photograph: Courtesy Gary
Long, W. M. Cline Company,
Vigo County Chapter
Daughters of the American
Revolution.

including chiefs of Indian tribes, with whom Harrison was in constant negotiation. The big house filled many functions: It was the governor's official dwelling, his office and military headquarters for the territory and a meeting place for the territorial council.

Governor Harrison called his house "Grouseland," because of the numerous small game birds found in the fields and meadows in the area. The grouse have long since left Vincennes but visitors to the house today can see models of them.

Governor Harrison's record at Vincennes was distinguished, marked chiefly by a series of successful negotiations with Indian tribes for the transfer of tribal lands. In 1805 the Treaty of Grouseland gave the United States title to all Indian lands in eastern Indiana. In 1809 another treaty, involving a payment of $10,000 to the Indians, transferred ten million acres of forest land to the government.

But Harrison's greatest achievement was a military one. In 1811 at the Battle of Tippecanoe on the banks of the Wabash north of Vincennes, Harrison, leading about one thousand troops, destroyed a stronghold of hostile and rebellious Indian tribes, followers of Chief Tecumseh. The victory and a boisterous campaign, for which the slogan was "Tippecanoe and Tyler too" helped elect Harrison President of the United States in 1840.

Governor Harrison left Vincennes and Grouseland in 1812, never to return. The territorial capital was soon transferred to Corydon, and a few years later Indiana became a state. Grouseland, no longer an official residence of importance, passed through many hands, suffered a century of neglect and decay. The once splendid grounds shrank to a small lot; the fine colonial porch and portico disappeared. A paper mill was built across the street in front of the house and the once wide view of the Wabash River was blocked by a high levee. Then, the house was acquired by the Daughters of the American Revolution through its Francis Vigo Chapter with the object of restoring it to the way it was when it was Governor Harrison's official residence.

The finest room in Grouseland is the parlor, which served Governor Harrison as an official council chamber. The portrait over the fireplace is of Governor Harrison. *Photograph: Courtesy Gary Long, W. M. Cline Company, Vigo County Chapter Daughters of the American Revolution.*

The patriotic pride of the Daughters of the American Revolution of Vigo County, Indiana, is suggested by this marker in front of the Harrison Mansion they restored, own and display. *Photograph: Courtesy Andrew Hepburn.*

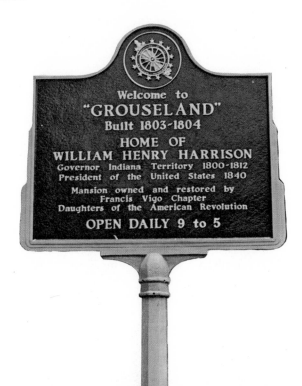

After years of careful research the restoration, which took several more years, was completed in 1970 and the house opened to visitors. They see a typical colonial mansion of classic elegance, with spacious, high-ceilinged rooms, filled with some original Harrison furniture, other pieces appropriate to the period and the celebrated portraits of Governor Harrison. One, by Rembrandt Peale, hangs in the handsome council chamber, with a center table that was an original Harrison possession. Tradition says that Governor Harrison and Chief Tecumseh negotiated a treaty while seated at it.

Grouseland is at the northwest corner of Park and Scott streets, and is best reached from Harrison Avenue. Its partially restored grounds are just south of the campus of Vincennes University, which Governor Harrison helped establish in 1806, the second oldest college in the Northwest Territory.

The Hermitage, Andrew Jackson Home, Nashville, Tennessee

More than any other American, Andrew Jackson personified the middle frontier, that vast new land of great forests and wide rivers extending west from the Alleghenies to the Mississippi. He first came to the frontier at the age of twenty-one, appointed as prosecuting attorney for the western district of North Carolina, which then included the present state of Tennessee. He had ridden across the mountains on a mare, carrying all his possessions which included a rifle, two pistols and half a dozen law books.

In October, 1788, he reached the settlement of Nashville on the Cumberland River, then a log-cabin town within a buffalo fence. From that time on Tennessee and the vicinity of Nashville was his home. He helped the frontier emerge from a forest wilderness, helped Tennessee become a state. He became its greatest citizen, its first representative in Washington, a U.S. senator, a military leader and hero—first of Tennessee, then of the nation— and finally, in 1828, the seventh President of the United States.

While a young man in Tennessee, Jackson engaged in the frontier practice of speculating in land, buying and selling many tracts. In 1804 he bought 420 acres on the Cumberland east of Nashville for $3,400. It was to become The Hermitage plantation and his home for the rest of his life.

When Jackson and his wife, Rachel, moved to The Hermitage it was little more than wilderness, only partially cleared. Their home was a cluster of log cabins, the largest a two-story blockhouse built to withstand Indian attack. Through the years The Hermitage, Andrew Jackson and the state of Tennessee grew together. As Jackson's fame and wealth increased The Hermitage grew in sophistication and elegance, the log cabins replaced by a typical plantation home, which in turn became a stately mansion of great charm. It was always Jackson's home and the home of his beloved Rachel. Both are buried in a templelike tomb on The Hermitage grounds.

The Hermitage, in Tennessee, a splendid Greek-Revival-style mansion, was the frontier home of a great soldier and President of the United States, Andrew Jackson. *Photograph: Courtesy Tennessee Department of Conservation.*

Today The Hermitage, maintained by the Ladies Hermitage Association and the state of Tennessee as a shrine and a memorial to Jackson, vividly reflects his character and tastes and in special ways tells the story of his extraordinary life. While The Hermitage was still a group of log houses Jackson, whose fame had spread beyond the borders of Tennessee, entertained distinguished guests there, including Aaron Burr and President James Monroe. It was to this frontier home that Major General Jackson returned, a national hero, after his stunning victory over the British at New Orleans, in 1814.

Soon, aided by a boom in the cotton market, he decided to build a bigger and finer house. His wife, Rachel, selected the site, a secluded meadow on Hermitage land. It was a comfortable but unpretentious house, which Jackson himself probably designed and had built by skilled slave labor under the direction of a master builder. Of burned brick it was rectangular in shape. Timbers used in the building were cut from Hermitage land. But compared to the log cabin home it replaced it was fine, indeed. Completed in 1819 the new Hermitage was the Jacksons' home for nine years. Then in 1828 Rachel died and Jackson was elected President of the United States.

Three years later Jackson, while President, made extensive changes at The Hermitage. Two wings and front and back porticos were added, a new kitchen and smokehouse were built, and the dining room enlarged to seat one hundred people. With Rachel dead Jackson brought Sarah York Jackson, wife of his adopted son, Andrew Jackson, Jr., to The Hermitage as its mistress. It has been suggested that the remodeling done was intended as a wedding gift to her.

But the remodeling didn't endure. In the fall of 1834 a fire destroyed The Hermitage except for some exterior walls.

Though he could ill afford the cost Jackson decided to rebuild The Hermitage and by a stroke of fortune chose as builders a gifted team of contractor-carpenters, Joseph Reiff and William Hume. It was fortunate too, that at the time the rebuilding began, the most favored style of domestic architecture was the classic and charming Greek Revival style. The mansion Reiff and Hume built—The Hermitage that visitors see today—exhibits major elements of Greek Revival style, including two-story porticos front and rear, each with six white Doric columns. With most of the furnishings from the older house destroyed by the fire, Jackson ordered new furniture from Philadelphia, had it shipped by sailing vessel to New Orleans and brought to Nashville by river steamer. The furniture cost $6,500. General Jackson lived in the remodeled and refurnished Hermitage until his death in 1845. He was buried in the garden next to the grave of Rachel. Eleven years later the estate was conveyed to the state of Tennessee by Andrew Jackson, Jr., with Jackson heirs and descendants continuing to live in the house as tenants at will. Some of them are buried in The Hermitage gardens, including the last, Andrew Jackson IV, who died in California in 1953.

The Ladies Hermitage Association, which now controls and exhibits The Hermitage under authority of the State of Tennessee, took over the

The graceful spiral stairway in the wide central hall is one of the unique features of the mansion. The ornately pictorial wallpaper was specially designed for the hall. Photograph: Courtesy Ladies Hermitage Association.

estate in 1889 in order to "beautify, preserve and adorn the same throughout all coming years, in a manner most befitting the memory of that great man, and commensurate with the gratitude of his countrymen." They have fulfilled their trust so well that visitors to The Hermitage now see the mansion and its extensive grounds about as they were during the last years of General Jackson's life, when, after his return from the White House and the Presidency, The Hermitage became a mecca for visitors from everywhere.

The mansion has a kind of quiet splendor. Most of the eleven rooms, besides kitchen, pantry, storeroom and cellar are spacious with high ceilings. They are filled with furniture acquired both in General Jackson's time and in later years when the house was the home of his heirs. All over the house are souvenirs and relics of Jackson's years as a military leader and as President of the United States. Family portraits are everywhere. Two interior features, both in the wide central hall on the first floor, are unique. One is the graceful spiral stairway, suspended from a semilunar rear wall, and the other is the wallpaper of the central hall, bought in 1835 during the final rebuilding of the mansion. Ornately pictorial—it depicts the legend of the travels of Telemachus in search of his father, Ulysses—it is one of the few examples of historic scenic papers preserved in the country.

The formal development of the grounds began in 1819 when the first new Hermitage was built. Then General Jackson engaged an English gardener, William Frost, to lay out the grounds. The result was a superb lawn shaded by great trees, and to the east of the mansion an orderly acre of flowers, arranged in a formal pattern.

The extensive grounds of The Hermitage, as well as the house, vividly evoke the life and character of General Jackson and his wife, Rachel.

Though the beautifully maintained grounds are worth seeing, the focus of interest for most visitors is the tomb of General and Mrs. Jackson, a circular, templelike building. In the surrounding burying ground many members of the family are buried.

Several buildings of special interest are scattered over the grounds. One is a log cabin, part of the cluster of log buildings that were the home of the Jacksons from 1804 to 1819. Another log cabin was the home of Uncle Alfred, General Jackson's favorite house servant, who was born on the plantation in 1803 and lived there until 1901. Maintained as an exhibit building on the grounds is the Jackson coach house, with a coach used by Jackson as President for trips to and from Washington, along with other relics of Jackson's travels and of his great interest in horse racing.

A museum on the grounds, developed in a building that was once used by servants, is filled with thousands of examples of Jacksoniana.

The Hermitage is easily reached. It is thirteen miles east of Nashville, just off US 70 N, a few miles north of Interstate 40 between Nashville and Lebanon. The wide channel of the Cumberland River is just north of it. The mansion and grounds are open to visitors from 8 A.M. to 6 P.M. during summer months; 9 A.M. to 5 P.M. the rest of the year.

Though Andrew Jackson's Hermitage is Greek Revival in exterior style, some of the rooms suggest the Victorian taste of its owner.
Photograph: Courtesy Ladies Hermitage Association.

The handsome furniture of the big dining room was bought for the house in Philadelphia about 1835. Portraits include those of General Jackson and his wife, Rachel, his adopted son and wife, Sarah. *Photograph: Courtesy Ladies Hermitage Association.*

132

Focus of interest is the templelike tomb
and monument where General Jackson
and his beloved wife, Rachel, are buried.
Graves of other members of the Jackson
family are nearby. *Photograph: Courtesy
Ladies Hermitage Association.*

Abraham Lincoln Birthplace, Hodgenville, Kentucky

In about 1800 Thomas Lincoln, an itinerant carpenter and farmer, settled in the frontier village of Elizabethtown, Kentucky. Eight years later, after marrying an Elizabethtown girl named Nancy Hanks, he paid $200 in cash for a three hundred-acre tract a few miles southeast of Elizabethtown, and there built a one-room log cabin. A special lure of the new land was a splendid, big, limestone spring called Sinking Spring. Thomas Lincoln built his primitive house conveniently near the spring. An enormous oak tree stood on the boundary of his land. About a year later, on February 12, 1809, Thomas Lincoln's wife gave birth to a child who was named Abraham for his grandfather. The date of his birth is now a national holiday because the child became one of the greatest of Americans, the martyred Civil War President of the United States.

The child Abraham lived in the cabin at Sinking Spring only two and a half years. Then, perhaps because of a dispute over the title of the land, the family moved to another farm in Kentucky, and afterward crossed the Ohio River into Indiana, where young Abraham grew from boyhood to manhood.

The history of the birthplace cabin at Sinking Spring was shrouded in doubt and mystery for many years. No one considered it important until after the child born there had become President of the United States. Then the cabin, or at least a cabin believed to have been the birthplace, became involved in an extraordinary series of events. In 1861 a neighboring land-owner named Rodman decided the cabin was worth preserving, bought it and moved it to his own farm, where it remained until 1894 when a New Yorker bought the birthplace farm and moved the cabin back to its original site. In succeeding years the cabin was dismantled, logs carefully marked and moved to a series of expositions.

For a time the cabin was stored in the basement of a house on Long Island, New York. But it was not abandoned there. While the cabin languished in a basement a campaign was launched to build a suitable national memorial that would have the Lincoln birthplace at its core. By 1905 enough money had been raised to buy the birthplace farm and four years later the cornerstone of the memorial was laid, with President Theodore Roosevelt delivering the address. Two years later the impressive memorial was finished: an ornate, templelike building with an imposing façade of Doric columns standing at the head of a long flight of steps. There are selected words of Lincoln and exhibits of Lincoln's life inside. The memorial's principal exhibit is the tiny, shabby little log cabin where Lincoln was born. Seeing it there, after exposure to the grandeur of the memorial building, is a shock to many visitors. The cabin is only twelve feet wide, seventeen feet long and eleven logs high. Space between the logs is chinked with clay. The floor is of clay and the single entrance door is so low that most visitors must stoop to enter it. The interior is dim and grim. Most would call it unfit for human habitation.

This massive, ornate memorial building shelters a unique national shrine—the tiny, shabby one-room log cabin where Abraham Lincoln was born on February 12, 1809. *Photograph: Courtesy National Park Service.*

An artist with an eye for
accuracy helped restore the
Abraham Lincoln birthplace
cabin to its original setting
among fine old trees near a
big spring on the frontier of
western Kentucky.
*Photograph: Courtesy
National Park Service.*

McGuffey Birthplace, Dearborn, Michigan

About the time Abraham Lincoln's father was moving to western Kentucky, a group of Scotch-Irish migrants from eastern Pennsylvania moved west over the mountains and settled in the wooded Allegheny foothills just east of the Ohio River, south of the frontier village of Pittsburgh. One of the group, Alexander McGuffey, had been an Indian fighter and scout for Anthony Wayne. There in a log cabin in September, 1800, Alexander and his wife, Anna Holmes, had a son they named William Holmes, second child in a family that would have eleven children.

Two years later Alexander McGuffey moved his family west again, across the Ohio River into a newly opened wilderness region where for $500 he bought 165 acres of forest land and began to convert it into a primitive farm. William Holmes and his brother and sisters grew up there. The boy had a prodigious memory, read every book he could find and as opportunity permitted attended frontier schools. As he grew older he began teaching in country schools between intervals of attending college at Washington College, Washington, Pennsylvania, from which he graduated in 1826. The same year he was elected to the faculty of Miami University at Oxford, Ohio, on the western edge of that state.

In the years that followed McGuffey began a project that would make both him and Miami University famous. He wrote a series of school readers completely different in pattern and concept from any written before. The first, appearing in 1836, was an immediate success. A slender little book of eighty-four pages, it was called the *McGuffey's New First Eclectic Reader.* Over the next twenty years McGuffrey wrote six readers while he moved from one professorial position to another, including the presidency of two Ohio colleges, and finally a faculty position at the University of Virginia at Charlottesville, where McGuffey moved in 1845. He lived there until he died in 1873.

But before Professor McGuffey died in Virginia his readers had attained a success greater than any books ever published in America. They were used in the schools of thirty-seven states and by the end of the nineteenth century more than 125 million copies had been distributed. The name "McGuffey Readers" was a household word. In them, one writer said, "a child could find a code of social behavior to carry him through any experience." Mark Sullivan in his *Our Times* (New York: Charles Scribner's Sons, 1927) says of them: "Their moral and cultural influence on two generations of Americans was incalcuable."

One young American who gained almost all his formal education from *McGuffey Readers* was a Michigan boy named Henry Ford. As a man he frequently mentioned that McGuffey had given him almost all his formal education. He regarded McGuffey as one of the greatest Americans, ranking him with Lincoln and Washington, and for years as he built up his automotive empire at Dearborn, Michigan, Ford thought of someday providing a suitable memorial to McGuffey.

In 1930, Henry Ford found
the one-room log cabin on a
western Pennsylvania farm
where William Holmes
McGuffey was born in 1800.
Ford moved the cabin to
Dearborn and had it restored
as a memorial to a great
teacher. *Photograph: Courtesy
Henry Ford Museum and
Greenfield Village.*

138

The interior of the McGuffey birthplace has been modified enough to permit its use as a primary school, where selected pupils learn from *McGuffey Readers*. Enlarged illustrations from the readers are on the walls. *Photograph: Courtesy Henry Ford Museum and Greenfield Village.*

The opportunity came about 1930 when Ford began to develop the remarkable collection of historic dwellings and other buildings that he called Greenfield Village. He decided that McGuffey's birthplace belonged there. But no one knew just where McGuffey had been born, except that it was in western Pennsylvania. Ford engaged a team of investigators to scour the region and locate the cabin, if it existed. They finally reported that a tiny, one-room decrepit log cabin on an abandoned farm near Claysville was probably the McGuffey birthplace.

That was enough for Henry Ford. In 1931 he bought the farm, carefully moved the little cabin to Dearborn and reassembled it in Greenfield Village, where it is seen today by the multitudes of visitors who flock through that unique assemblage of historic buildings dedicated to the American past.

Appropriately, Mr. Ford converted the little cabin to a school, where selected children of the Dearborn region could learn to read, of course using *McGuffey Readers* as their texts. On the birthplace farm Mr. Ford erected a suitable granite memorial to McGuffey. Other memorials were established at Miami University where work on the readers had begun, but the birthplace cabin at Greenfield Village is the one that most vividly evokes an understanding of William Holmes McGuffey as the most influential teacher this country has produced.

Booker T. Washington Birthplace, Virginia

In 1856, from his home in Springfield, Illinois, Abraham Lincoln was engaged in a political campaign that would make him President of the United States. An important issue in that campaign was the freedom of Negro slaves. In 1856, there was a frontier plantation in the Blue Ridge foothills of southwestern Virginia, owned by a John Burroughs. It contained about two hundred acres, most of them cleared, a primitive plantation of log buildings including several one room cabins where the few slaves Burroughs owned lived. In one of those cabins, in 1856, a child was born named Booker, who for twelve years was known only by this name. A few years later on a property inventory of the Burroughs plantation, he was listed as: "One negro boy, Booker, $400."

Booker was nine years old and a good worker and field hand when, in 1865, the ten Burroughs slaves were told that they were no longer slaves, but, thanks to Mr. Lincoln, free.

For the boy Booker, the early years of freedom were grueling. For a pittance in pay he worked long, exhausting hours in a coal mine and at a salt furnace. But, during those years, from some deep inner resource he developed a passion for learning. He taught himself spelling from a borrowed copy of *Webster's Spelling Book*. When he was about twelve he entered a neighborhood elementary school and acquired a last name. The teacher asked his name and he answered with pride: "Booker Washington."

When he was about sixteen, Booker heard about a new school at Hampton Institute, a school for Negroes. He walked the five hundred miles to Hampton, working at odd jobs along the way. At Hampton his prodigious appetite for learning flowered. He not only learned to read, but read widely. He developed such a reputation as an orator that two years after he left Hampton Institute, he was invited to return to deliver a postgraduation address. He called it "The Force that Wins." The speech so impressed the directors of Hampton that he was offered a faculty position, and two years later he was chosen to establish a normal school (a two-year school for teach-

In 1856, a slave boy named Booker was born in a one-room log cabin on a plantation in western Virginia. The cabin, now restored, is a national shrine. *Photograph: Courtesy National Park Service.*

ers) for Negroes in Alabama. It became Tuskegee Institute, the most famous and influential of all Negro schools. As its head Booker T. Washington, the former slave boy, became nationally renowned. He was an advisor to Presidents of the United States on racial matters and political appointments. His great ability as an orator made him a regular speaker. He delivered hundreds of addresses, wrote thirteen books, including his autobiography, a national bestseller, *Up From Slavery*. When he died in 1915 Tuskegee Institute owned 107 buildings and two thousand acres of land. Now a fully accredited college it has more than three thousand students and numbers among its alumni some of the most renowned and successful Negroes in the country.

Belated recognition of Booker T. Washington (he added the middle initial "T" when he learned that his mother wanted to call him Booker Taliaferro), and his greatness as an American came in 1957 when the two-hundred-acre Burroughs plantation was acquired as a national monument, and a log cabin, possibly the birthplace of the child Booker, was restored. Other frontier log buildings of the plantation were also restored, rail fences rebuilt and the surrounding fields reestablished to look as they were when the boy Booker worked in them as a field hand.

The birthplace and the typical frontier plantation of which it is a part are maintained by the National Park Service, with 218 acres within the monument limits. It is reached easily from Roanoke, Virginia, sixteen miles south on Virginia Highway 116, then six miles east on Virginia 122. The monument is open every day during daylight hours.

Kit Carson Home, Taos, New Mexico

Most settlers on the frontier sought to tame and convert the wilderness. Kit Carson, short for Christopher, born in 1809 in a settler's cabin on the forest frontier of western Kentucky, was an exception. All his life he followed the frontier, moving west with it, leading expeditions through it, fighting and subduing Indians. During the course of a unique and extraordinary career that brought him fame, he was a trapper, buffalo hunter, guide, soldier, Indian agent and one of the picturesque Mountain Men who led wagon trains through the wild western mountains.

Throughout his life he had only one home, an adobe house in the high, beautiful mountain village of Taos, New Mexico. He bought the house as a wedding present for his bride in 1843 and lived there until he died in 1868. Today the house is one of the distinctive showplaces of Taos, preserved as a memorial to Kit Carson, maintained much as it was when Kit and his wife, Josepha Jaramillo, and their children lived there.

Kit Carson was an original. His career, in the sense of heroism and adventure, was epic. When he was a small child his family moved west from Kentucky to a town on the Missouri frontier that was an outfitting point for wagon trains using the Santa Fe Trail. There at the age of sixteen, because he could "shoot straight, drive a team, hunt Buffalo," Kit was accepted as a

Restoration was extended to the plantation where the cabin stands, including the split-rail fences, corn patch and orchard trees.
Photograph: Courtesy National Park Service.

In 1843, Kit Carson, Indian fighter and scout, soldier and renowned frontiersman, bought a primitive adobe house in the mountain village of Taos, New Mexico. It was his home for the rest of his life.
Photograph: Courtesy Kit Carson Memorial Foundation.

Life in Kit Carson's home combined
Spanish, Indian and the primitive
frontier elements as this view of the
family kitchen suggests. *Photograph:
Courtesy Kit Carson Memorial
Foundation.*

member of an expedition led by Charles Brent, who would become the first
territorial governor of New Mexico, and Kit's best friend.

In time the caravan reached the tiny Spanish village Fernandez de Taos,
high in the forested Sangre de Christo Mountains, one of the oldest and
most picturesque communities in the country. It would be Carson's home
town the rest of his life, base for innumerable expeditions. There, though
he never learned to read or write English, he learned Spanish and Indian
sign language.

Within a few years Kit was an experienced Mountain Man, tracker,
guide and buffalo hunter, his reputation spreading steadily throughout the
West and then through the nation. Reports made by such explorers as John
Frémont, for whom Carson several times acted as scout and guide, were
published, extolling Kit's skills and courage.

In 1843 Carson married Josepha Jaramillo, daughter of one of the
oldest and most important families of Taos. There, for the next twenty-five
years Carson reared his family, entertained the growing stream of friends,
Mountain Men, trappers, traders, soldiers and dignitaries who came to Taos

Oxcarts, following the old Santa Fe Trail over the western mountains, brought Kit Carson most of the furniture for the bedroom of his Taos home. *Photograph: Courtesy Kit Carson Memorial Foundation.*

to see him. Over the years he became a soldier of national renown, and reached the rank of general. But his biggest job was that of Indian agent. As such he quelled Indian uprisings and broke the war spirit of the hostile Apache and Navajo tribes. One incident in that period involved an Indian attack on Taos. During the attack Carson nailed the American flag to a high pole and stood guard with his friends night and day to protect it. As a result Taos today is one of the few places in the country where the national flag officially flies night and day, high above Carson's home town, his home and grave.

When Carson bought his Taos home it was about twenty-five years old, a primitive adobe dwelling typical of the Spanish frontier in the Southwest. Walls were about thirty inches thick, with small windows protected by wooden shutters. Ceiling beams were made of peeled round logs or *vigas,* cut in the nearby forest and then dragged to the site by oxen. Boards were laid on top of the *vigas* and about two feet of hard-packed earth spread over the boards as insulation. Floors were packed dirt. There was a fireplace in the corner of most rooms like those early Spanish settlers found in the dwellings

of the Pueblo Indians. In the kitchen was a big bell-shaped cooking stove called a *flagon de campana*. No one seems to know how many rooms were in the original house, but in Carson's day there were at least ten, spread around three sides of a large patio. Like many Spanish houses the patio was a prime living area, with beds of flowers, a well and a beehive-type oven called a *horno*.

After acquiring his house, Carson began to make improvements and changes, putting glass in the windows, wooden floors over the packed earth and covering the insulating earth on top with a sloping wooden roof, eventually faced with roofing paper.

Following the death of both Carson and his wife in 1868, the historic house was sold and passed through various hands, growing progressively more shabby until about 1950 an organization called the Kit Carson Memorial Foundation was organized to acquire and restore the house. Later the house was declared a national historic site.

The region around Taos was scoured to find original Carson furniture. Several rooms were refurnished as nearly as possible to the way they were when the Carson family lived there. Other rooms are maintained as museums, each devoted to aspects and periods of the Southwest important in Carson's life. There is a Spanish room, an Indian room and an Early American room. The colorful patio is again almost exactly as it was during Carson's day. The old house evokes Kit Carson in dozens of special ways, through its

148

pictures, souvenirs, relics, weapons, documents and clothing. Though other Carson memorials are nearby—the Kit Carson Memorial State Park with Carson's grave and the American flag flying day and night over it, and the nearby Carson National Forest—the old house tells Kit's story best and helps visitors understand why one friend called him "not a great man, but a great character," and another, "simple as a child, brave as a lion." The house is open to visitors daily. They can find it just east of the town plaza on Kit Carson Avenue.

Sutter's Fort, Sacramento, California

The restored patio is colorfully decorated with native flowers and relics of pioneer life. *Photograph: Courtesy Kit Carson Memorial Foundation.*

Spanish and Russian settlers had been developing the region of California for a good many years before that remarkable land became a state. They came by ship and by migration from the south, established their communities and named most of the features of the land. Then, starting about 1830, soon after a revolution in Mexico had lost California to Spain, pioneers began reaching California from a new direction: the East. Led by fur traders and trappers, they scaled the awesome ramparts of the High Sierras and began to trickle down into California's rich, fertile central valley.

After 1839 most of them set their sights on the most eastern outpost of civilization in central California, where most immigrant trails converged. They knew it as Sutter's Fort, built in 1839 by a remarkable man, Captain John Augustus Sutter. Born of Swiss parents, he became one of the earliest and most influential American settlers in California.

Sutter's Fort was a real fort, guarded by high adobe walls on which cannon were mounted. It stood on a knoll overlooking the American River, near that stream's junction with the larger Sacramento River. Almost immediately after its completion the fort (also Sutter's home) became a goal for travelers who trekked west over the mountains: fur traders and explorers and settlers bound for new lands. It offered everything they needed, in addition to sanctuary. There they found much needed supplies, a tannery, a distillery and a blacksmith shop. Sutter's industry was legendary. What he didn't have within the walls of his fortress-home he maintained within the forty-eight thousand-acre Spanish grant of which Sutter's Fort was the core. He had sawmills, herds of cattle, irrigated land and ran a steamer down the Sacramento to San Francisco Bay. Sutter's generosity and hospitality to westbound travelers, often exhausted and penniless, was a byword.

Energetic and imaginative, Sutter built his wilderness empire with ingenuity. When, in 1841, Mexican pressure forced the Russians (who had settled on the northern California coast) to abandon their settlement at Fort Ross, he bought door frames from them, which had been made in Norway and brought around the Horn by ship, for his new home. He also bought twelve Russian cannon that he mounted on the walls of his fort on the Sacramento.

Fort Sutter was guarded by a private army of about fifty well disciplined

Indians. About twelve of them were Sutter's personal guard, wearing gaudy uniforms of blue or green cloth trimmed with red, also bought from the Russians.

One of the most powerful landowners and traders in the West, Sutter was active in the rapid development that followed control of California by the United States. After the Mexican War, U.S. forces were stationed at his fort during the 1846–47 conquest of California. In 1849 he was a member of the Constitutional Convention that resulted in the admission of California as the thirty-first state.

But before that an event occurred which profoundly affected Sutter and his fort on the Sacramento. With the rapid increase in migration to California Sutter saw the need for more lumber, and in order to obtain it engaged a millright named James Marshall to build a sawmill on the American River some miles east of Sutter's fort. The mill went into operation in January, 1848, and some days later Marshall found a nugget of gold in the millrace. Marshall reported his find to Sutter and both men decided to keep

Sutter's Fort, frontier fortress, home and wilderness outpost now in the heart of modern Sacramento, was once a goal for immigrant trains into California. *Photograph: Courtesy California Department of Parks.*

▷

Exhibits of the restored Donner Fort at Sacramento, now an historic memorial, relate to pioneer days. This one helps tell the grim Donner story. *Photograph: Courtesy California Department of Parks.*

SURVIVORS OF THE DONNER PARTY

the discovery secret. It was history's worst kept secret, and triggered the country's biggest and most famous gold rush. Within a short time central California from the mountains to the sea swarmed with gold seekers. The mountain slopes bloomed with gold camps. San Francisco, before the gold strike a sleepy Spanish settlement called Yerba Buena, became a roistering boom city.

Captain Sutter's fort at the newly surveyed village of Sacramento was a focal point in this frantic activity. The first gold had been found on his land in the mountains. Hordes of prospectors stopped there for outfitting on the final stage of their rush to the gold camps to the East. Men were becoming immensely rich from the gold. Sutter should have been one of them, but he wasn't. Ironically, the gold rush resulted in his losing almost everything. His guards and staff deserted for the mines. Indian laborers became drunken delinquents. Many who stopped for outfitting stole his property or forgot to pay. He was soon bankrupt. In a futile effort to retrieve his fortune he tried his hand at prospecting, then went east to obtain congressional confirmation of his Mexican land grants. He failed. He died impoverished at Lititz, Pennsylvania, in 1880.

For many years after Sutter left his fort and home in the growing community of Sacramento the historic cluster of buildings within their high adobe wall was neglected and fell into decay. Then in about 1890 increasing public interest in the historic site resulted in its acquisition by the state of California which made it a state historical monument. Complete restoration was ordered.

Now fully restored within a public park at 28th and L streets, east of Sacramento's imposing Capitol building, the old fort draws a steady stream of visitors. They see Sutter's living quarters as he used them, his offices, an assortment of shops and workrooms, the cannon bought from the Russians, the Indian guard room, an extraordinary collection of relics of pioneer days as diverse as prairie schooners, and the spurs of pony express riders, California's first iron printing press, an assortment of documents and prints, and life-sized models of Sutter and Marshall inspecting a model of the golden nugget that brought fame and wealth to California and ruin to the unfortunate owner of Sutter's Fort.

VI

CIVIL WAR PERIOD HOMES

A climax in the settlement of the West came with the discovery of gold in California followed by the rush of eager gold seekers into the far West. Thousands made the journey by land and sea, transforming a region of vast cattle ranches and sleepy Spanish villages into the thirty-first state with a population that trebled within ten years.

But within a few years after the discovery of gold in California the focus of history shifted to the East. For years there had been ominous rumbles of discord and dissent between the states of the North and the South over slavery in the southern states and the right of those states to maintain this institution. The issue became acute during the election of 1860 when an Illinois lawyer, Abraham Lincoln, who lived in Springfield was the candidate of the new Republican party. Lincoln won the election and left his Spring-field home for Washington never to return. Within weeks the dissension between the North and South exploded into civil war, a long, bitter and bloody struggle. Houses that had significant association with the war and the men who represented conflicting forces are described in this chapter. They include the modest Victorian house in Springfield where Lincoln lived; a handsome mansion in Arlington, Virginia, that had been the home of the great leader of the southern Confederate armies, Robert E. Lee; a mansion in Richmond, Virginia, capital of the Confederate states, where the President of the Confederacy, Jefferson Davis, made his wartime home; a farmhouse in the rolling hills of eastern Virginia where the war ended with the surrender of General Lee to the Union leader, General Grant, and a modest brick house in Washington, D.C., the home of a tailor, in which President Lincoln, shot by an assassin, died.

Lee Mansion, Arlington, Virginia

One of Washington, D.C.'s splendid vistas extends from the Lincoln Memorial south across Arlington Memorial Bridge to a slope of tree-shaded lawn studded with white gravestones to the crest of a hill and the pillared façade of a handsome mansion. The hill slope and the graves are part of the world's most famous burying ground, Arlington National Cemetery. The mansion at the crest of the hill is variously called the Lee Mansion, the Custis-Lee Mansion and Arlington House. One of the historic houses of America it stood on its commanding hilltop long before graves of the nation's military dead and celebrated citizens surrounded it. It was the home, for many years prior to the Civil War, of Robert E. Lee, one of the most distinguished Americans and, some say, the nation's finest soldier.

Many of the hundreds of thousands who each year wander over the paths and drives of Arlington National Cemetery and among its more than 140,000 graves take time to visit the Lee Mansion. Some of the cemetery's most celebrated graves are near it. Those of the late President John F. Kennedy and his brother Robert are just below the mansion. Major Pierre L'Enfant is buried a few feet from the front portico, near the grave of General Philip Sheridan, the brilliant Federal Cavalry leader whose most important opponent in the Civil War was the soldier who made his home at Arlington House and left it to lead the armies of the Confederacy.

Visitors to Arlington House, or the Lee Mansion, find nothing there to suggest war and death and burial. Instead they see a superbly beautiful dwelling, a memorial not only to General Lee and his family, but to George Washington and his heirs. One of them, George Washington Parke Custis, grandson of Martha Washington, built Arlington House.

That was in 1802, the year Martha Washington died. Her grandson began building Arlington on land that had been left him by his father. It was understood that the house was to receive the legacy of his grandmother including furniture, pictures and other possessions from Mount Vernon, as well as many of George Washington's personal effects. As a result, no other house in America, except Mount Vernon, has more association with George Washington.

George Washington Parke Custis, builder of Arlington House, was a talented artist and naturally selected a gifted architect to design his home, a young Englishman named George Hadfield. The result, an adaption of the classic Greek tradition, was spectacular, with a façade dominated by a portico sixty feet wide behind a row of six massive Doric columns supporting a classicly simple pediment. Identical wings extend on either side of the main façade so that the entire front of the house extends 140 feet.

The mansion was a family residence for sixty years. During that period it was the setting for a series of notable events. In 1824 it was visited by General Lafayette, who said that the view from the portico was the finest he had ever seen. Six years later on June 30, 1831, the family room of the mansion was the setting for the wedding of Mary Anne Randolph Custis, only daughter of the builder, to Lieutenant Robert E. Lee, recent West Point graduate and one of the celebrated Virginia Lees. His family and the Washington Custis families had been associated for two generations. After the wedding Arlington House became the Lee home. Six of the seven Lee

Surrounded by the graves of the nation's military dead, Arlington House, the home of General Robert E. Lee, looks north toward the Potomac River and Washington. *Photograph: National Park Service.*

children were born there, and Lee rising steadily through Army ranks, always returned to Arlington from military assignments.

The final and perhaps the most poignant of all events associated with Arlington House occurred in April, 1861. During a secret meeting held in Washington Colonel Lee had been offered command of the then developing Union armies. Tradition says that he returned to Arlington, where, sitting in his bedroom he pondered his decision for hours. He finally decided that he could not forsake Virginia in the contest that was beginning. Two days later he left Arlington House, never to return, and went to Richmond to accept a command in the Confederate Army. Mrs. Lee stayed at Arlington briefly to dismantle the household and ship its possessions south.

Within months Arlington's acres became buffer land in the strategic defense of Washington against the expected Confederate attack. Arlington mansion became a military headquarters for the general in charge of the southern rim of fortifications. In 1864, when Mrs. Lee was unable to pay taxes levied on the property it was confiscated by the government, and about two hundred acres of the estate set aside for a national cemetery.

For years after the Civil War, as Arlington Cemetery grew slowly to its present size of about five hundred acres, its graves increasing by thousands, Arlington mansion was an empty shell, an office for the superintendent of the cemetery and a storehouse for his tools. During those years rights to the estate were contested by a Lee descendant, following the death of General Lee in 1870 and Mrs. Lee in 1873. A lawsuit over the ownership was settled in 1883 with the government paying $150,000, but it was many years before the unique character of Arlington House as an historic site and memorial was recognized. In 1925 the Secretary of War, under whose jurisdiction the mansion was maintained, was authorized by Congress to begin restoration, and to search for furniture known to have been in the house. Much of it was found and returned, and replicas of pieces not found were made. In 1933 jurisdiction over Arlington House was transferred to the Department of Interior, and in 1955 was made a national memorial, to be administered by the National Park Service.

Under that agency's management the mansion has been beautifully restored and is exhibited. Tours are maintained under direction of carefully trained guides. Rooms and associated accessories of special interest to visitors include the family parlor where Lee was married which contains several of the general's most personal possessions; the handsome dining room, with a portrait of the builder and much of the original Lee family china, glassware and silver; the thirty-seven-foot high central hall, with a hanging lantern copied from one in Mount Vernon, a portrait of General Lee's father, General Light Horse Harry Lee and hunting-scene murals painted directly on the plastered walls by Arlington's first owner.

Of special interest upstairs is the bedroom of Colonel and Mrs. Lee, where six of the Lee children were born, and where Colonel Lee made his fateful decision to resign from the Union Army.

Visitors may also explore the grounds, now restored to their condition when Colonel Lee was the master of Arlington. Outbuildings include the smokehouse, summer kitchen, icehouse, toolhouse and stable. Just north of the mansion is a small but excellent museum. Both the flower and kitchen gardens of the estate have been carefully restored. But the unique and most spectacular feature of the grounds is a great tree, a towering, splendid Himalayan cedar.

Arlington House, easily discovered by any visitors to Arlington Cemetery, is accessible both by footpath and driveway, with parking areas adjacent. It is open to visitors 9:30 A.M. to 6 P.M. spring and summer months; the rest of the year until 4:30 P.M.

Abraham Lincoln Home, Springfield, Illinois

The only home Abraham Lincoln ever owned was in Springfield, Illinois. When he bought it in 1844, Springfield was little more than a village on the edge of the emerging frontier, and Lincoln, thirty-five years old, was a small-town lawyer, married just two years. When he left his Springfield home seventeen years later, he had been elected President of the United States. The house today, maintained by the state of Illinois almost exactly as it was when Lincoln lived there with his family, is a poignant and intimate memorial.

For the first two years of their marriage the Lincolns lived in Springfield boarding houses, or at the Globe Tavern, where board was $4 a week. But after the birth of their son, Robert Todd, Lincoln, whose reputation as a lawyer was growing steadily, decided that his family needed a better place to live. So he bought a one-and-a-half-story cottage within easy walking distance of his law office. The cottage cost $1,500 along with the small town lot where it stood. The house, built in 1839, had been the home of the Reverend Charles Dresser, the Episcopal rector who had married Lincoln and Mary Todd in 1842.

Over the years that followed, as the Lincoln family grew and Lincoln himself emerged on the national scene, the house too grew and changed. Changes involved building a brick foundation wall for a wooden fence along the front of the house, a high board fence connecting with a carriage house at the rear, and later the enlargement of the house to two full stories. It was painted Quaker brown and was similar in style to hundreds of Victorian houses built throughout the Midwest during the middle decades of the nineteenth century. The enlargement cost $1,300.

The Lincolns *needed* a larger house. Three of their four sons were born there, Edward Baker, "Eddie," in 1846, William Wallace, "Willie," in 1850, Thomas, "Tad," in 1853. Eddie died in the house. But even with the extension to a full two stories the house was just barely large enough for the family. There were five bedrooms, including a maid's room, upstairs and five rooms, including a kitchen, downstairs. Furnishings were without pretense. Many pieces were classically Victorian in style, though others were of an earlier,

The only home Abraham
Lincoln ever owned was built
in 1839 in Springfield,
Illinois, a typically Victorian
house. Lincoln bought it
in 1844, left the house in 1861,
never to return. *Photograph:
Courtesy Illinois Division of
Parks.*

The dining room furniture
was mostly cherry wood, made
by craftsmen of the region.
*Photograph: Courtesy
Illinois Division of Parks.*

simpler period made by the frontier craftsmen of the region. The most elegant room was, naturally, the front parlor.

That room, and the adjoining back parlor, increasingly became settings for significant events. There in May, 1860 Lincoln received the committee appointed to notify him formally of his nomination for the Presidency. Throughout the campaign that followed, the house was a frequent setting for political strategy meetings, and following the election the house was filled for many hours of the day and often well into the night with well-wishers and office seekers. On the last full day that the Lincolns occupied the house, February 6, 1861, they held a grand public levee, with thousands of people thronging through the house to meet the President-elect and Mrs. Lincoln.

The next day the Lincolns left the house for the last time to take the train for Washington. Standing on the rear platform of the train Lincoln made a brief but moving speech to friends and neighbors gathered at the train to wish him Godspeed, a poignant farewell to his home, his town and friends. In it he said in part: ". . . To this place and the kindness of these people, I owe everything. Here I have lived for a quarter of a century and have passed from a young to an old man. Here my children have been born and one is buried. I now leave, not knowing when, or whether ever, I may return. . . ."

He did return to Springfield four years later, but not to his home there. He came back, amid the grief of a nation, surrounded by funereal pomp, to be buried in a Springfield cemetery, where an ornate monument marks his grave. On it is a tablet with the full text of his farewell to his home and his friends.

The history of the Lincoln house in Springfield following the President's assassination includes occupancy by several families before it was acquired by the state as a gift from Robert Todd Lincoln. Before he left for Washington, Lincoln, expecting to return to Springfield eventually, rented the house for $350 a year to Lucian Tilton, head of the Great Western Railway. Following the assassination the Tiltons continued to live in the house until 1869. Other families leased the house until, in 1883, it was rented by Osborn H. Oldroyd who turned it into a Civil War museum with a display of Lincolniana. In 1887 Oldroyd persuaded Robert Todd Lincoln to give the house to the state of Illinois.

Over a period of several decades, the state of Illinois collected original Lincoln furniture from various museums and private collectors, with the result that visitors, thousands of them each year, now see the house as it was during the Lincoln family residency. One of several Springfield exhibits relating to Lincoln's life, it is at Eighth and Jackson streets, in the heart of present-day Springfield, open to visitors every day.

Mrs. Lincoln's bedroom was austerely simple in appointments. *Photograph: Courtesy Illinois Division of Parks.*

The master bedroom was
Mr. Lincoln's. At the tilt-top
desk between corner windows,
Lincoln wrote speeches that
have become famous.
*Photograph: Courtesy
Illinois Division of Parks.*

▷

The twin parlors are crowded
with pieces of Victorian
elegance, and were frequent
settings for political and
social occasions during the
last years the Lincolns lived
there. *Photograph: Courtesy
Illinois Division of Parks.*

White House of the Confederacy, Richmond, Virginia

Unlike Washington, D.C., which was planned as a nation's capital, Virginia's historic city of Richmond had been settled for more than a hundred years when the Civil War began and the city became the capital of the Confederate States. There was no official residence for the President of the Confederacy, Jefferson Davis, and his family. So in June, 1861, the city of Richmond bought a handsome private mansion near the state capitol and tendered it to Jefferson Davis as an official home. For almost four years after that the fine house was Jefferson Davis' official residence and the meeting place for his cabinet, and ever since has been known as the White House of the Confederacy.

The house, actually white, and in some ways suggesting the official residence of the President of the United States in Washington, D.C., had been built by a Richmond banker named John Brockenbrough in 1817. To design and build his mansion Brockenbrough chose Robert Mills, leading architect of his day and designer of many public buildings and monuments throughout the nation. Mills was an exponent of the Classic Revival style, applying it to the Brockenbrough house with impressive results. The mansion's most notable feature was a two-story Doric portico behind eight columns. Interior rooms were high-ceilinged, spacious. At the beginning of the Civil War it was one of the finest dwellings in Richmond, a suitable residence for the President of the Confederacy. The city paid $42,984.97 for the house, furnished it with handsome Victorian pieces and established the President's office and cabinet room on the second floor. For several years frequent receptions were held, particularly during the early years of the war, when the hopes of the Confederacy, following a succession of victories over the Union armies, were rising. They were gay and brilliant occasions attended by everyone not in mourning.

But with the beginning of the siege of Richmond in 1864, the house became a somber place, visited by sharp tragedy when President Davis' five-year-old son fell to his death from the high porch of the mansion. Then, less than a year later President Davis and the entire Confederate government left Richmond, leaving their White House to the disposition of the rapidly advancing Union armies.

With the war over the once splendid mansion became a military headquarters, housing Union Army officers assigned to direct the affairs of District Number 1, the state of Virginia. Later, growing steadily shabbier and neglected, it served briefly as a public school, until in 1894 it was rescued from complete ruin by the Confederate Memorial Literary Society.

The society began to slowly restore the mansion and established it as a museum, a treasure house of Confederate history, filled with relics of the Confederate period and the Civil War. Now officially known as the Confederate Museum it is open to visitors. It contains the world's largest and finest collection of Confederate and Civil War relics, including the sword

Typically Greek Revival in style, the White House of the Confederacy had been the handsome home of a Virginia banker before becoming the official residence for the President of the Confederate States, Jefferson Davis. *Photograph: Courtesy Virginia State Travel Service.*

and uniform worn by General Robert E. Lee when he surrendered the Army of Virginia to General Grant at Appomattox Court House, along with a large collection of battle flags, uniforms, weapons and military equipment used by the soldiers of the South.

Many visitors find their highest interest in several handsomely refurnished rooms set with fine Victorian pieces, presumably appearing as they might have appeared during the brief years of glory when the mansion was at the core of the Confederate States of America.

In the heart of downtown Richmond, the house is at 1201 East Clay Street. It is open to visitors from 9 A.M. to 5 P.M. weekdays, and on Sunday afternoons.

McLean House, Appomattox, Virginia

In the spring of 1865 General Grant's stubborn aggression against the Confederacy paid off. Early in April the Confederate defense lines around Petersburg and Richmond collapsed. General Lee gathered weary remnants of his once proud Army of Northern Virginia and started plodding west from Richmond with well-equipped Union troops pressing hard from the rear and Union cavalry leader Philip Sheridan charging to cut him off.

Of the approximately twenty-seven thousand men marching with Lee only about eight thousand were fit to fight, and they had scant ammunition or supplies. But General Lee had two desperate hopes: First to reach Appomattox Station, east of Lynchburg, where he expected to find a trainload of supplies, then to march west to join General Johnson in the mountains.

But on April sixth Sheridan's cavalry caught up with Lee's army and dealt it a shattering blow, capturing thousands of Confederate soldiers and most of Lee's meager remaining supplies.

In the meantime General Grant and General Lee had been in touch by dispatch, Grant urging Lee to surrender at once and so avoid further bloodshed, Lee temporizing in the hopes of salvaging some remnant of Confederate pride.

Straight ahead in the path of the slowly advancing armies of the South and North lay a cluster of houses and other buildings scattered over a few acres of rolling farmland. Typical of many farm settlements of the region it was almost too tiny to be called a village. But it had a name, Appomattox Court House. It was a county seat boasting a jail. There was a tavern and general store and about six houses. From the settlement the smoky ranges of the Blue Ridge Mountains, with Lynchburg at their base, rose about thirty miles to the west. Three miles southwest, on the railway, was Appomattox Junction, where General Lee had directed that several carloads of desperately needed supplies be sidetracked to await his arrival.

The most substantial house in Appomattox Court House was the home of William McLean and his family, a solid, two-story brick house, with a pillared porch. There were slave quarters and outbuildings on the sides and rear. In front of it ran the Richmond–Lynchburg stage road.

The McLean House at Appomattox Court House, typical farmhouse of western Virginia, acquired instant fame when General Lee there surrendered his army to General Grant. *Photograph: Courtesy National Park Service.*

McLean had been a successful planter near Manassas, Virginia, when the war began. There his fields were engulfed in the first Battle of Bull Run, and sometime later he decided to move to the hills "where the sound of battle would never reach them." So in 1863 he bought the plantation at Appomattox Court House. It seemed improbable that the war would bother him there. But it did in an extraordinary way. For all practical purposes it ended in his house.

While General Grant and General Lee were exchanging inconclusive dispatches, General Sheridan settled matters decisively. On April ninth he won the race to Appomattox Court House, seized the Confederate supplies waiting there for General Lee's arrival, and threw an unbreakable barrier of troops in front of Lee's army, now completely bottled up, hungry and bone weary.

So General Lee sent General Grant a request to talk surrender. The dispatch reached Grant while he was away from his headquarters, but he immediately headed for the proposed rendezvous, Appomattox Court House.

Lee and a member of his staff arrived first and selected the McLean House as the meeting place. They were accompanied by a member of Grant's staff, Colonel Babcock, who had brought word that General Grant was hurrying to the meeting. The three men settled down to wait in the pleasant Victorian parlor of the house.

Soon there was a sound of boots clumping up the steps to the porch and General Grant, accompanied by General Sheridan and a cluster of staff officers, came in to what would become one of the most memorable meetings of all time. Every detail of it has been recorded many times: the aspect of the room, the look and character of the men who filled it, what they said and did. What they did ended the Civil War.

There were three tables in the room, a small round marble-topped table at which Grant sat, another small table with a square marble top where General Lee sat and a larger wooden table where General Grant's assistant adjutant general, Joe Bowers, established himself to make notes. There were not enough chairs in the room for all the officers attending Grant, so most of them waited on the porch.

The appearance of the two leaders was in striking contrast. General Lee, famed for his impeccable attire, was particularly splendid in a new uniform, crimson sash and jeweled sword, his boots gleaming. General Grant, who had a reputation for being casual about his dress, was unusually so. His uniform was dusty, with pants tucked in muddy boots. He had no sword or sidearm. He had come from the field, without returning to his headquarters. In any case his baggage had been lost. Later Grant admitted that as he hurried to the meeting he did think that his appearance might affront General Lee, that he was "afraid Lee might think I meant to show him studied discourtesy." But General Lee had no such reaction.

The meeting, the only occasion during the long and bitter war when the two leaders met face to face, began casually. Grant and Lee recalled incidents during the Mexican War when they had served together. General

An artist who was not there used inaccurate imagination in creating this painting showing the historic surrender in the parlor of the McLean House at Appomattox Court House. The original can be seen at the Visitor Center. *Photograph: Courtesy Virginia State Travel Service.*

Grant brought his officers in from the porch and introduced them to General Lee.

Then the business of the day began. Lee asked Grant to tell him the surrender terms. Grant did, and Lee was surprised and pleased, since they were far more generous than he had expected. The terms were that all men were to be paroled, officers signing paroles for the enlisted men. The men were to go home and they would be disqualified from taking up arms again. Only public property would be surrendered. Officers would retain their side-arms and horses.

General Lee quickly agreed to the terms and General Grant then made a written copy of them in his order book and handed the book with its penciled copy of the terms to General Lee to read. Except for minor changes in language Lee agreed and the terms were written in final form.

General Lee then raised one final point. He said that many of the enlisted men were using their own horses, which would be of great value to the men in reestablishing their homes. Grant gave orders to exempt the horses if claimed by the riders as their own. He also gave Sheridan orders to distribute twenty-five thousand rations to the half-starved Confederate soldiers. Ironically, they came from the supplies that Sheridan had seized a few hours earlier.

General Lee gave General Grant a formal note of acceptance, and the meeting ended. Word of the surrender spread like wildfire among the troops camped not far away. General Grant's soldiers jumped up and down with excitement, played their bands, fired salutes, demonstrations that General Grant quickly stopped, saying: "War is over, the Rebels are our countrymen again."

Both generals then left with their staffs for their respective head-quarters, Grant's about a mile west of Appomattox Court House, Lee's about a mile east. But before separating they agreed to meet at the village again. They did so the next day, sitting on horseback alone, on a little knoll over-looking the Appomattox River, a few hundred yards east of the McLean House. They talked about a number of things, particularly General Grant's desire to have Lee meet President Lincoln.

Three days after the meeting at the McLean House the formal and physical surrender of the Army of Northern Virginia occurred at Appomattox Court House, within sight of the McLean House where the surrender terms had been arranged. There, in a triangle formed by the meeting of three highways the Confederate soldiers stacked their arms. General Gibbon, assigned to supervise the surrender, telegraphed the surrender statistics to General Grant: twenty-five thousand to thirty thousand men, 147 cannon, ten thousand small arms, seventy-one flags.

After the surrender the McLeans returned to their home, lived there for another four years, then moved to Alexandria, Virginia. Because their house had become famous, and a place of public curiosity, speculators bought it in 1893, planning to take it apart and reerect it in Washington as an exhibit. The project failed. Souvenir hunters stole much of the dismantled house and weather destroyed the rest.

170

A Union Army photographer took
this photograph of the McLean
House soon after General Lee surrendered there to General Grant. The
photograph later helped the National
Park Service rebuild and restore the house.
Photograph: Courtesy National Park Service.

A few years ago Congress established the Appomattox Court House Historical Park and directed that the National Park Service restore the village and rebuild the McLean House. It was done with the aid of photographs and descriptions made at the time of the surrender. Core of the exhibit area is the parlor where the surrender terms were made, restored to appear almost exactly as it was at the time of the meeting there. The rest of the house, in no way involved in the surrender, has been fully restored as a typical Victorian dwelling of the period. The restored courthouse is now a visitor center, where exhibits vividly detail events leading to the surrender and the surrender itself. One of them, an historic painting, shows a romanticized meeting between General Grant and General Lee. They are seated at a small wooden table with thirteen staff officers looking on. Park historians at the McLean House correct the inaccuracies of the painting with their story of the famous meeting.

The historical park is easily reached. It is on Virginia Highway 24, three miles northeast of that highway's junction with US 460, the main highway between Lynchburg and Richmond, about twenty-two miles east of Lynchburg. It is open to visitors during daylight hours, every day except Christmas.

House Where Lincoln Died, Washington, D.C.

In 1849 a Swedish tailor named William Petersen built a house on Tenth Street in the northwest section of Washington, D.C. It was a narrow four-story house of brick, like dozens of others built in Washington at the time. The lower floor, where Petersen had his tailoring shop, had a step-down entrance. The family lived on the three upper floors and occasionally rented extra rooms.

Across the street from the Petersen house theatrical producer John Ford built a theater in 1863. Two years later it was Washington's finest and largest center for theatrical entertainment. Until the spring of 1865 there was no association between the handsome, popular Ford Theater and the simple house of tailor William Petersen across the street.

Then in April, 1965, Ford's Theater and Petersen's house became linked in one of the nation's most poignant and bitter tragedies. In the theater, on the night of April 14, 1865, President Abraham Lincoln was shot and mortally wounded by John Wilkes Booth. Nine hours later the President died in the house across the street. Since then both the Ford Theater and the house where Lincoln died have been restored to the way they looked on the fateful night of April 14, 1865, and are maintained under the administration of the National Park Service as unique and dramatic memorials to Abraham Lincoln.

The story of the Petersen house is this: With war imminent and soldiers crowding into Washington, Petersen found it profitable to rent spare rooms to Union soldiers quartered in the city. One of his rooms, a small back bedroom was rented to William T. Clark, a former member of a Massachusetts regiment who was then working at the quartermaster general's office. The room was normally used by Petersen's daughter, Pauline, then away at boarding school.

Usually Tenth Street, on the eastern edge of Washington's general business district, was a quiet street. But on nights when Ford's Theater staged a performance it was often crowded with theatergoers, noisy with their talk and laughter.

On the night of April 14 the theater was presenting a celebrated comedy, *Our American Cousin*. It was an appropriate presentation, for the nation was in a mood to be happy. Five days earlier General Grant had accepted the surrender of the Army of Northern Virginia from General Lee, at Appomattox Court House. And President Lincoln, who liked the theater as much as anyone, was also in a mood to relax. It was announced that he would attend the theater that night with Mrs. Lincoln and some friends, and a special box was reserved for them. General and Mrs. Grant were invited to join the theater party, planned as a kind of victory celebration, but at the last moment the general was called away from Washington by an urgent family crisis.

So the theater crowd on Tenth Street and the noise they made were probably greater than usual that night. It is likely that Petersen from an upstairs window of his house saw the presidential party arrive at Ford Theater and heard the crowd cheer the President. That was about eight o'clock in the evening. About two hours later, shortly after ten o'clock, near the end of the third act of the play, Petersen, if listening, must have heard the pandemonium at the theater and then, a little later, could have seen President Lincoln leaving the theater, carried on an improvised stretcher, across the cobblestoned street and up the steps to his, Petersen's, house. The President was alive, but Dr. A. F. A. King, and other physicians who examined him, knew that moving the dying President over the rough cobblestones to the White House would have been fatal. The doctors ordered the stricken man taken to the nearest bed, which was a back bedroom of the Petersen house. The bed in the room was narrow and, because of his great height, too short for the President, so he was laid diagonally across it.

From that moment, the little back bedroom of the Petersen house and the house itself became the focus of intense interest, the most important dwelling in the country, perhaps in the world. As word of the attempted assassination spread, every man of prominence then in Washington flocked to the house, filling all its rooms and overflowing into the street where a great crowd stood throughout the night. In a front parlor Mrs. Lincoln, occasionally going to the bedside of her dying husband, stricken with grief, sat with friends. In an adjoining room Secretary of War Stanton questioned witnesses to the shooting, while Corporal James Tanner took notes. Also in the house were members of the Cabinet, top military leaders of the Union forces and many others. They included newspaper and magazine writers and artists, who that night and the next day, in long dispatches to their

journals, noted everything about the house in words and pictures. One of these was John Littlefield, an artist for the New York *Herald* and *Leslie's Weekly*. He made careful notes and sketches, later converting them to an extraordinary painting of the room where Lincoln lay dying. It showed Mrs. Lincoln bowed in grief beside her husband and twenty-two of the nation's leaders clustered about the bed where the President lay.

Lincoln died in the Petersen house at 7:22 A.M. on April 15, his death announced with the words of Secretary Stanton: "Now he belongs to the ages." Soon after that the President's body was taken from the Petersen house to begin a long and solemn pilgrimage: First the body lay in state at the White House where funeral services were held on April 19, then was transferred to the rotunda of the Capitol where the casket was viewed by vast throngs. A slow journey on a crepe-decked funeral train began on April 21, with the body placed in state in several large cities en route. The burial took place on May 4 in Lincoln's home town, Springfield, Illinois.

Following the President's death the Petersen house continued to command attention. Crowds of people flocked to Tenth Street and stood long hours in front of the house and Ford's Theater. Some writers and artists were admitted and visited the rooms associated with the death of the President and made notes. As a result the Petersen house became for a time one of the most familiar houses in the country, with every detail of decoration and furnishing described.

It also became a difficult house for William Petersen to maintain as his home and tailor shop. He died a few years after the assassination and in 1876 heirs of the Petersen family sold the house for $4,500 to a Louis Schade, who edited a newspaper, the Washington *Sentinel*. For many years he ran a print shop and publishing office in the basement and lived in the upper floors. Then, in response to public interest, the government acquired the house in 1896 and for some years used it to house an extensive collection of Lincolniana and Civil War relics that belonged to Osborn H. Oldroyd, at the time the most notable collection of its kind in the country.

Actual restoration of the house as a Lincoln shrine did not begin until 1928 when various patriotic societies began the slow job of reassembling the original furniture or duplicating it, and restoring the house to its condition when President Lincoln died there in April, 1865. The job was completed by the National Park Service, which now maintains the house and exhibits it.

The task of restoration, particularly the room where Lincoln died, was greatly aided by reference to the famous Littlefield painting which originally appeared in *Leslie's Weekly*. Furnishings in the room are either the originals or exact duplicates of the originals: The too-narrow and too-short bed is a copy of the original one, but the pillow on it is the same one on which the President's head rested while he lay dying. The rug and wallpaper are copies of the originals. The washstand and other accessories are either exact copies or the original ones. Even the pictures on the walls are the same: Rosa Bonheur's *Horse Fair* and the *Village Blacksmith*.

The same fidelity does not extend to all the restored rooms of the house.

Following Lincoln's assassination at Ford's Theater across the street in April, 1865, this modest house in Washington, D.C., has become a poignant shrine to Lincoln's memory. At the time of Lincoln's death, it was the home of a tailor named William Petersen.
Photograph: Courtesy National Park Service.

Furniture from Lincoln's home in Springfield replaces some that was in the Petersen house at the time of the assassination, but it is similar in design, particularly the high-backed rocking chair in the front parlor where Mrs. Lincoln rocked and grieved. At the back of the house is a wide parlor, added after the tragedy, which houses part of the Oldroyd collection. Here are displayed the celebrated and moving Littlefield painting and other relics of the assassination day. Other relics and souvenirs have been established in the basement of the restored Ford Theater across the street, including the murder weapon and a series of audiovisual projections that show and describe great events of Lincoln's life with moving eloquence.

Most of the thousands of visitors who flock to the house where Lincoln died, wisely visit first the beautifully restored Ford's Theater across the street, where it takes little imagination to understand the step-by-step sequence of tragedy that occurred there on that April night in 1865. Then, when they cross the street, visitors follow in the steps of the men who carried Lincoln into the Petersen house. Both the theater and the Petersen house are open to visitors every day except Christmas.

VII

HOMES OF WRITERS, ARTISTS, INVENTORS

One of the most fruitful and creative epochs in the history of the country started not long after the beginning of the nineteenth century and continued for many decades. It coincided with a period of great national expansion and industrial development. Not since the flowering of the Renaissance in Italy has such an army of creative men produced as many important books or as many great works of art, invented so many useful appliances, processes and machines.

Some of these writers, artists and inventors built or acquired notable houses. A selection of the most important and interesting of their houses is described in this chapter: a quaint and charming dwelling near Tarrytown, New York, where the gifted teller of tales Washington Irving lived for many years; an eccentric mansion in Hartford, Connecticut, which the greatest American humorist Mark Twain designed for himself and his family; a hilltop house and great studio called Chesterwood in southwestern Massachusetts where Daniel Chester French lived and created such immortal sculpture as the Lincoln figure in the Lincoln Memorial in Washington, D.C.; a Victorian mansion in New Jersey where the world's most renowned and prolific inventor, Thomas Edison, lived for many years. Each of the four famous houses is now a state or national memorial, filled with examples of these great men's work.

Sunnyside, Washington Irving Home, Tarrytown, New York

One of the most charming and remarkable dwellings in the country was for many years the home of a most charming and remarkable American. The house is Sunnyside and it overlooks the Hudson River in Tarrytown,

New York. Sunnyside's owner was Washington Irving, popular American writer of his time as well as one of the most gifted literary craftsmen. Popular both in this country and abroad, he was as much at home in London and Madrid as in New York. But from 1835 until his death in 1859 his home was at Sunnyside. Few dwellings anywhere more completely reflect the taste and character of their owner.

Sunnyside, and the estate which it dominates, exist today almost exactly as they were during the last years of Washington Irving's life. It is crowded with his possessions arranged and displayed as he wanted them, thanks to meticulous restoration and maintenance provided by the Rockefeller-endowed foundation, Sleepy Hollow Restorations.

Washington Irving was born in New York City in 1783, eleventh and youngest child of Scotch-English parents. His father, a prosperous merchant, made sure that his youngest son had advantages. They included the first of a series of trips abroad when he was twenty-one years old. When he returned to New York Irving studied law but soon abandoned it for his first love, writing, a talent to which he brought polished style, a robust imagination and a delightful sense of humor. Before he was thirty he had written *Knickerbocker's History of New York,* a massive project called "the first great book of comic literature produced by an American."

Not long after its publication Irving went to England to run the London branch of his family business. It soon failed and, out of necessity, Irving turned to writing as a fulltime vocation, with impressive results. Book after book followed, one of which, *The Sketch Book,* contained two of the stories on which much of his popularity rests, "Rip Van Winkle" and "The Legend of Sleepy Hollow."

Both were stories of early Dutch life along the Hudson River, a region and a period that fascinated Washington Irving, accounting for such delightful characters as Ichabod Crane, the Headless Horseman and the Van Tassel family. It was perhaps Irving's preoccupation with Dutch life and manners that led to his acquisition of the Sunnyside property.

In any case, in 1835 Irving acquired twenty-four acres on the banks of the Hudson near the Dutch settlement of Upper Mills, now Tarrytown. The land had been part of the vast Philipsburg estate, one of the largest and most notable of the Dutch Hudson River holdings. Irving had known the region since childhood and was delighted with its romantic character, ancient forests and little rivers winding down to the Hudson River from rugged hills. It was the Sleepy Hollow region that Irving made famous and it is still famous because of him.

The land acquired was part of a farm that had been owned by a branch of the Van Tassel family Irving immortalized in "The Legend of Sleepy Hollow." On it was a small Dutch farmhouse, which Irving converted to Sunnyside. Over a two-year period he completely remodeled and extended the farm cottage, converting it into a remarkable dwelling. It had no special architectural style and represented no precise period of design. There were stepped Dutch gables, Gothic windows and many details that were pure Washington Irving, such as weathervanes from old New York buildings and

Whimsical and charming, Washington Irving's Sunnyside home on the Hudson River resembles a Grimm's fairy tale castle. *Photograph: Courtesy Sleepy Hollow Restorations.*

interior arches and alcoves. To help him Irving enlisted the advice and suggestions of friends, including a neighbor, George Harvey, who was a notable architect.

Soon, Sunnyside, which Irving called his "elegant little snuggery," became a mecca for friends and relatives, whom Irving entertained with wit and style. So many came to visit that about ten years after the original remodeling Irving added a three-story tower with a sloping oriental roof to house servants and the overflow of guests. It was called the Pagoda.

Over the years Irving never stopped making changes and additions, so that toward the end of his life Sunnyside, though small looking was actually a substantial mansion of more than fifteen rooms in the main house and assorted outbuildings, including a greenhouse, stables, icehouse and two-level root cellar. Irving maintained the extensive grounds in a seminatural state. Features included splendid old trees, many of them huge, and a meandering stream with a waterfall, flowing through a pond which Irving called the "Little Mediterranean." There was a small gorge near the Hudson River, winding trails and walks bordered in season by a profusion of wild flowers.

Because of its character as a unique dwelling and the fame of its owner, Sunnyside soon became a favorite subject for artists such as the celebrated George Inness. Perhaps no private house in the country has been sketched, painted or photographed so often.

As maintained by Washington Irving the interior of the house both in design and furnishings was delightful, often a whimsical expression of Washington Irving's taste and reflecting all the periods of his life. Arrangements, though informal, were contrived with elegance. Details of Irving's own imaginative ingenuity included built-in closets (unusual for the time), barrel ceilings, arched alcoves and a bathroom with almost modern accessories.

Irving thoroughly enjoyed Sunnyside and made the remarkable house the center and core of his life. But he continued to travel, going to the American West to gather material for a series of books, and to Spain where he served as minister between 1842 and 1846. From each trip he brought back to Sunnyside rich and colorful accessories—glass, silver, ceramics, linen—much of it purchased in Spain, London and Paris. They are all now placed as Irving had them.

Washington Irving's library and study, seen just as he left it, is a treasure room of rare books, many of them unique. Photograph: Courtesy Sleepy Hollow Restorations.

Following Washington Irving's death in 1859 Sunnyside was occupied by two nieces who had often acted as his hostesses. But in 1896 another relative acquired the property, adding a large and inharmonious Tudor wing on the north side, razing some outbuildings and eliminating small rooms in the house. Members of the Irving family continued to own Sunnyside until 1945 when it was acquired by Mr. John D. Rockefeller, Jr. Opened to the public the next year, it was closed after a time following a decision to restore it as it was during the last years of Washington Irving's life. Several years of careful investigation, research and restoration of both house and grounds were completed in 1961, and Sunnyside was placed under the direction of Sleepy Hollow Restorations for public viewing and maintenance.

A reception center some distance from the house provides visitors with information on both Washington Irving and Sunnyside and provides trained

guides for tours of the house and grounds. Rooms of notable interest include Irving's study, often used as a one-room apartment. There is a fireplace, huge desk, a large collection of souvenirs and relics of his long and beguiling life and walls lined with books. The study is across the hall from an elegant dining room which adjoins a parlor with a rosewood piano, where Irving's nieces played, sometimes accompanied on the flute by Irving himself. A curious downstairs accessory was a bathroom, the only one in the house. The walls of the house are crowded with an extensive collection of prints, paintings, sketches, framed documents and photographs. One room is a small picture gallery, the walls hung with framed original illustrations from many of Irving's books. The final and superb restoration of Sunnyside extended to the grounds and outbuildings, now almost exactly as they were during Irving's life.

Though Sunnyside is open year round, it is best visited during the spring and summer, when flowers and trees are at their romantic best. A vast and spectacular wisteria vine that drapes itself over the front entrance and the west wall is almost a symbol of Washington Irving's own colorful life and romantic tastes, which Sunnyside preserves and exhibits as the unique and delightful home of a unique and delightful man.

Entrance gates to the Sunnyside estate are on the west side of US 9 about two miles south of the village of North Tarrytown. The estate is open to visitors on weekdays from 10 A.M. to 5 P.M., April to mid-November; the rest of the year, from noon to 4 P.M.

By mid-nineteenth-century standards, the kitchen of Sunnyside had the most modern accessories, a wood-burning cooking range and hot water heater. *Photograph: Courtesy Sleepy Hollow Restorations.*

Mark Twain House, Hartford, Connecticut

Mark Twain was a wanderer. Humorist, satirist, storyteller, gifted wielder of words, he spent much of his long and richly patterned life roaming the world, with no home to call his own. Born in 1835 he spent his boyhood in the frontier village of Hannibal, Missouri, on the Mississippi River. He was early infected by the virus of wanderlust. It led to his becoming a journeyman printer, a Mississippi riverboat pilot, a miner, a newspaper reporter. As a reporter he became renowned as a humorist and storyteller, gained fame, wealth, a wife and family and for seventeen years a house and home.

The house was one of the most extraordinary dwellings ever built in Hartford, Connecticut, which Twain (of course his real name was Samuel Clemens) described as "one of the most beautiful towns it has been my fortune to see." He had been married in 1870, relatively late in life (he was thirty-five years old), soon after the publication of *Innocents Abroad*. A huge success, the book made him instantly famous and steadily richer. So he moved to Hartford where his publisher had an office and in 1873 began building a house which he planned as a permanent home for a growing family. The lot selected was on a fine residential street that was lined with stately houses, some owned by Twain's friends. Twain described his lot as ". . . a sightly

The most elegant room was the big dining room where the author entertained a stream of friends. *Photograph: Courtesy Sleepy Hollow Restorations.*

piece of land on Farmington Avenue . . . tableland sloping down to a pretty stream that wound through the willows and among the trees. . . ."

To design and build his new home he engaged a gentle and acquiescent architect named Edwin Potter, who tried to build what his client wanted. The result was a collaboration in which it is difficult to discover what each of the two men, the architect or owner, contributed. A reporter from a Hartford paper, invited to inspect the house as it neared completion, called it ". . . one of the oddest looking buildings ever designed for a dwelling. . . ." Other words of description equally appropriate might be eccentric, bizarre, rambling, whimiscal, unique. It was a big house of patterned brick, three stories high, with a forest of gables and towers, with chimneys rising from steep sloped roofs. Five balconies were tucked away in the gables. There was a huge irregular porch extending along two sides. Semicircular and octagonal bays projected from three sides. Interior details were as strange as the exterior. Many of the nearly thirty rooms, including an extensive kitchen and service wing, reflected some special desire or interest of the owner. Tiffany glass and black walnut woodwork were everywhere. Unusual features included a plate glass window directly over the fireplace in the dining room so, as Mark Twain said, "he could watch the flames leaping to meet the falling snowflakes." From the mahogany room, a huge and ornate downstairs bedroom (where a long list of rich and famous friends stayed) extended a dressing room designed to resemble the pilothouse of a Mississippi River steamboat. Another reflection of Twain's years as a riverboat pilot was the porch or *ombra* (Italian for shadow), which looked like the deck of a river steamer. The library, and family sitting room, boasted a huge fireplace with a carved mantel brought from Scotland. From the library extended a semicircular conservatory, designed and filled with growing things by one of Mark Twain's neighbors, Harriet Beecher Stowe, author of *Uncle Tom's Cabin*. Perhaps the most remarkable and famous room of the big rambling house was the billiard room, a huge balconied room on the third floor, where Mark entertained his men friends and did most of his writing.

Mark Twain and his family moved into the new house in 1874 and lived there almost continuously until 1891. There he did his best and most celebrated work, producing such books as *Tom Sawyer, Huckleberry Finn, A Connecticut Yankee* and *Life on the Mississippi*. The house became the social center of Hartford and was visited by streams of neighbors, friends and business associates. Twain and his wife filled the house with a vast assortment of things they liked, many collected from their travels—pictures, bric-a-brac, furniture, odds and ends.

Curiously, the remarkable house never acquired a special name, as did many of the great houses of the Victorian era. It was simply Mark Twain's house, and still is. Today, maintained by the Mark Twain Memorial, it reflects the boisterous, gifted, brilliant personality of its owner, his interests, hobbies and eccentricities.

While living in Hartford in the Farmington Avenue mansion Mark Twain began to engage in enterprises that eventually forced him to give up his home. He became a publisher, at first hugely successful because of the publication of the life of General Grant. He invented a typesetting machine and spent a fortune trying to perfect it. Both enterprises failed, plunging him into debt. Added to the cluster of disasters was a bitter blow in the death of his daughter, Susy. About that shattering event Twain wrote: ". . . spirits of the dead hallow a house for me. . . . Susy died in the house we built in Hartford. Mrs. Clemens would never enter it again. But it made the house dearer to me. I visited it once, since, when it was tenantless and forlorn, but to me it was a holy place and beautiful."

With Mark Twain and his family gone from Hartford, the house on

When viewing Mark Twain's new home in Hartford, Connecticut, a writer called it "one of the oddest looking buildings ever designed as a residence." Twain himself helped design the extraordinary house. *Photograph: Courtesy Mark Twain Memorial.*

Farmington Avenue lost nearly everything that made it fascinating and unique, except the oddity of its design. Various people lived there. It was rented briefly. In 1903 it was sold to Richard H. Bissell, president of the Hartford Fire Insurance Company, who lived there with his family until 1917. Then the house was rented as a private school for boys. The school moved in 1922, and the house entered a period of degeneration and neglect; it was used as a storage warehouse, then broken up into a series of separate apartments.

Meanwhile Hartford interests began to raise funds to acquire and restore the house, to refill it with the possessions of Mark Twain and his family. They succeeded in 1929. Since then the house has been substantially restored to its aspect during the seventeen golden years when Mark Twain and his family lived there. Most of the original family rooms are open to the public. A series of exhibits is maintained in the basement, including the typesetting machine that brought Twain disaster, along with other things that brought him pleasure, such as his bicycle and a Russian sleigh.

The extraordinary house, with a large share of its original grounds intact, is easily visited. On one of the best residential streets of Hartford, it is a few blocks west of the downtown area at 351 Farmington Avenue. It is open to visitors Tuesday through Saturday, from 10 A.M. to 5 P.M. and Sunday from 2 P.M. to 5 P.M.

Chesterwood, Daniel Chester French Home, Stockbridge, Massachusetts

More Americans have seen and remember the work of Daniel Chester French than that of any other sculptor. Many regard his heroic, brooding, Lincoln in the Lincoln Memorial in Washington, D.C., as the most moving statue anywhere. And every schoolboy is familiar with the figure of the Minute Man at Concord, Massachusetts, plow in one hand, gun in the other. There are many others, such as Columbia University's Alma Mater and the symbolic figures of the four continents at the New York Custom House.

But until recently few people knew about French himself, or where he lived and worked. Now they are beginning to associate his work and life by visiting Chesterwood, his hilltop house and studio in the Berkshire Hills of southern Massachusetts. In 1966 Chesterwood, which French developed from a farm in 1896, was made a national historic landmark. Later the home and adjacent studio, together with a museum converted from an old barn, were turned over to the Daniel Chester French Foundation and opened to visitors. Now, during summer months Chesterwood with its family home, huge and fascinating studio and sculpture museum barn are explored by an increasing number of visitors. They find the estate tucked away among forested hills, near Stockbridge.

The huge ornate mantel of the library was imported from Scotland, the semicircular conservatory at the end of the room was designed and filled with plants by a neighbor, Harriet Beecher Stowe. *Photograph: Courtesy Mark Twain Memorial.*

Mark Twain's bedroom, in his extraordinary Hartford, Connecticut, home, was cluttered with Victorian oddities collected during his travels, and included an enormous carved bed. *Photograph: Courtesy Mark Twain Memorial.*

Daniel Chester French was a Yankee to the core. Born in Exeter, New Hampshire, in 1850, he grew up in New England and spent more of his life there than anywhere else. Through generations of New England ancestors he was connected with renowned families such as the Whittiers and Websters. His father, a judge, served as assistant secretary of the treasury through three administrations.

When he was a boy Daniel's family moved to that most celebrated of New England's famous villages, Concord, Massachusetts, where a neighbor was Ralph Waldo Emerson (in time French would do a bust of Emerson). Another neighbor was Louisa May Alcott, artistic member of the talented Alcott family. She discovered young Daniel's latent talent for artistic expression, particularly sculpture, gave him a few lessons and loaned him modeling

Chesterwood, a mansion in Massachusetts, was the summer home and headquarters for many years of the renowned sculptor Daniel Chester French. *Photograph: Courtesy Mrs. William Penn Cresson.*
▷

For the formal garden adjoining his home, Daniel Chester French designed a sundial and stone benches. *Photograph: Courtesy Mrs. William Penn Cresson.*

188

tools. Soon Daniel launched himself on a career unparalleled in American sculpture. His years in Concord were providential as they led to his first important commission.

But first Daniel studied anatomy under William Rimmer at the Massachusetts Institute of Technology and spent a month in the New York studio of J. Q. A. Ward (who did the celebrated Wall Street statue of George Washington). French returned to Concord in time to attend a meeting of village selectmen who were trying to choose a suitable memorial for a centennial celebration of a date in April, 1775, when Minutemen of the region soundly whipped British redcoats and started the Revolutionary War. French, then twenty-two, turned up at the meeting with a sketch of a statue he proposed to execute if he could get $400 for expenses. It seemed a good idea to Daniel's neighbors.

The statue was completed and erected at the end of the famous Concord bridge in time for dedication and unveiling on April 19, 1875, before a crowd of ten thousand people including President Grant. Ralph Waldo Emerson delivered the dedicatory address. In time the Minuteman statue became one of the most familiar monuments in the country, a symbol on defense bonds and postage stamps and pictured in school books. It was Daniel's springboard to fame and success. Ironically he did not attend the Concord ceremonies since he had gone to Italy to spend two years working in the Florence studio of Thomas Ball.

Not long after his return from Italy he found himself swamped with commissions and a stream of sculpture began pouring from his studio: statues of famous men, memorials, equestrian figures. Generally recognized as the most profoundly American of all sculptors, he divided his time among Washington, a fertile source of commissions, Boston and New York, where he maintained a studio in Greenwich Village. But he was not satisfied with the New York studio, particularly for summer work, and wanted a bigger and better one somewhere in the hills of New England.

So in the summer of 1896, French and his wife took a horse and buggy tour of western Massachusetts looking for a farm to buy. He found one among pleasant hills west of Stockbridge, about two hundred acres of hill land, with meadows, woods, a small house, a big barn, orchards and a splendid view.

The following year, with the help of an old friend, architect Henry Bacon, he built the kind of studio he wanted. He moved the barn some distance from the house and used its foundations for the studio, a remarkable building, specially designed to make the creation of massive works of sculpture as practical as possible. The main studio was a perfect cube, thirty feet in each dimension, with a peaked ceiling set with skylights that flooded the interior with light. There were special features—a casting room, and for the first time in any sculpture studio a railway track in the floor on which a platform traveled. It permitted the opening of thirty-foot-high doors in order to move models into the garden where they could be viewed from all sides.

French went to work in the new studio almost before the stucco on the exterior walls was dry. From it came statues, memorials and busts for a generation. Among the first was the equestrian figure of General Washington that now stands in Paris; three bronze doors for the Boston Public Library; the four continent figures for the New York Custom House; a statue of Emerson for the public library of Concord; Columbia University's Alma Mater.

While all this work kept him occupied, French still found time to build a new house, the present mansion of Chesterwood, replacing the small farmhouse he found inadequate. Again his friend Bacon helped with the design, a three-story stucco house of seventeen rooms, with a fine terrace across the front, modified colonial in design. The living room was an exact copy of the parlor in the Chester, New Hampshire, home of French's grandfather, Daniel French, attorney general of New Hampshire. He filled the house with antiques, many pieces with family association, and hung the walls with an extensive and valuable collection of paintings and prints.

Almost exactly twenty-five years after completing his studio, French was associated with Henry Bacon in another project, the Lincoln Memorial in Washington, D.C. Bacon was chosen as designer, French selected to execute the great seated figure of Lincoln which dominates the interior of the memorial. The memorial was completed in 1922. The Lincoln statue with its moving and eloquent solemnity, established French as one of the great sculptors of all time.

Until his death nine years later at the age of eighty-one, French continued to spend his summers in Chesterwood and his winters in New York, working much of the time, creating more notable figures and memorials. He died at Chesterwood on October 7, 1931. Thereafter the estate became the home of French's daughter, Margaret French Cresson. In 1955 Mrs. Cresson opened the studio to the public as a museum, exhibited there models and casts of many of French's famous statues and memorials. In 1963 the old barn was converted to a sculpture gallery where exhibits of New England artists, many of them friends of French, could be held. A few years later the estate was made both a national historic landmark and a Massachusetts historic landmark. The studio and about 150 acres of woods, laced with trails and gardened areas, was maintained by the Daniel Chester French Foundation as a permanent museum and exhibit area open to the public. The estate mansion, still the home of Mrs. Cresson, is open only by special arrangement.

Visitors find greatest interest in the studio, filled with models of the sculptor's work, and dominated by a model of the great Lincoln statue in Washington. Tools of the sculptor's craft are on tables as he left them. Other models are in the nearby sculpture barn or stand in the gardened grounds or on the porches of both the house studio and sculpture barn.

Chesterwood is open to visitors during summer months from 10 A.M. to 5 P.M. It is off Massachusetts Highway 183, one and a half miles south of that highway's junction with highway 102, south of Interstate 90 and west of Stockbridge.

A sculpture barn at
Chesterwood, converted from
a hundred-year-old farm
barn to an exhibition center
for art objects created by
Daniel Chester French as well
as by his sculptor friends.
*Photograph: Courtesy
Mrs. William Penn Cresson.*

◁

Two models of Daniel
Chester French's most
celebrated masterpiece—the
great Lincoln statue for the
Washington, D.C., Lincoln
Memorial—dominate one end
of the sculptor's huge studio
at Chesterwood. *Photograph:
Courtesy Mrs. William Penn
Cresson.*

Glenmont, Thomas Edison Home, West Orange, New Jersey

In 1886, seven years after he invented the first practical electric light, and four years after he ushered in the electrical age with the opening of the Pearl Street station in New York, first commercial distribution of electricity in the world, Thomas Edison, a widower, married for the second time. Thirty-nine years old, Edison was rich and famous. Everywhere he was known as the "Wizard of Menlo Park," where for many years he had maintained a laboratory out of which had come hundreds of revolutionary inventions.

As a wedding present Edison gave his new wife, Mina Miller, from Akron, Ohio, a fine new house. Called "Glenmont," it was a handsome mansion of twenty-three rooms surrounded by thirteen acres of landscaped grounds in an attractive residential district of West Orange, New Jersey. The house would be Edison's home for forty-five years, until his death in 1931, and Mrs. Edison's home until she died sixteen years later. While living at

The Edisons' favorite room was a huge second-floor living room. Edison called the big table at the left his "think bench." *Photograph: Courtesy National Park Service.*

An exact copy of the original, called the Black Maria, is a tarpaper-covered shack, within the grounds of the Edison Laboratory, near his home at West Orange. The original was the first motion picture theater in the world. *Photograph: Courtesy National Park Service.*

Glenmont Edison perfected devices and processes that resulted in more than five hundred patents, most of them developed at a complex of laboratories he established in 1887, about a mile east of the Glenmont estate. Both the estate itself, maintained almost exactly as it was during the many years Edison lived there, and the laboratory center are now a national historic site, maintained and exhibited by the National Park Service.

Glenmont was no ordinary big house. It was palatial, built by a New York executive six years before Edison bought it. He spared no expense to build his house, either in its construction or furnishings. Only the finest materials were used—bluestone block from Connecticut, pressed brick of special quality from Baltimore, Wyoming freestone for the stone trimmings, massive solid oak doors, a grand staircase of mahogany. The most luxurious and expensive fabrics were used in draperies, rugs and wall coverings. All of which may account for the fact that not long after its completion the house was up for sale, along with all its splendid appointments, and the original owner bankrupt.

Mrs. Edison was delighted with the new house and its extensive grounds and gardens, and gradually began to supplement its elegant appointments with a thousand and one souvenirs of her life with the genius who was her husband: family portraits and gifts from important people all over the world. Three Edison children were born at Glenmont, Madeleine and two sons— Charles, who became Secretary of the Navy and governor of New Jersey, and Theodore, a scientist like his father.

Visitors to the house today see it almost as it was when Edison died in an upstairs bedroom in 1931. His son Charles once said of the house where he spent his boyhood: "In its truest sense Glenmont is like Emerson's definition of an institution—it is the lengthened shadow of a man."

Most visitors find greatest interest in the second-floor library and living room, the Edisons' favorite room, spacious with big picture windows. There are more personal relics of the Edison life here than in any other room, including a big flat-topped desk which Edison called his "thought bench," and where he claimed he conceived many of the things that would be developed and patented from his nearby laboratory. Of the many hundreds, the most important was the motion picture camera.

Other notable rooms in the house include a reception room on the ground floor with a small pipe organ that Edison liked to play and a formal drawing room with yellow damask-covered walls that adjoined a conservatory filled with growing things. A notable accessory in the handsomely paneled dining room is a cabinet filled with one of the Edisons' prized possessions, an exquisite collection of Venetian glass.

Most visitors to Glenmont also explore the nearby laboratory complex, which Edison called his "invention factory." There, he said, he and his staff could "build anything from a lady's watch to a locomotive." Maintained as exhibits at the laboratory are innumerable examples of Edison's inventive genius, either originals or exact copies, ranging through the whole spectrum of electrical, mechanical and chemical development. There is a huge library with more than ten thousand volumes relating to scientific and industrial research, along with Edison's three thousand four hundred laboratory notebooks extending over sixty-one years of inventing, as well as original copies of 1,093 patents granted to Edison. A unique personal exhibit in the laboratory library is the cot where Edison occasionally napped while working round the clock.

Of special interest at the laboratory is a precise reproduction of the "Black Maria," a tar-paper shed used by Edison as the first motion picture theater. It now serves as a theater where visitors may see motion pictures relating to Edison's life and achievements.

The Edison National Historic Site is easily reached. Site headquarters is at Main Street and Lakeside Avenue, West Orange, New Jersey, two miles west of the Garden State Parkway, north of Interstate 280. Glenmont is about a mile west of Main Street on Park Way. The laboratory is open daily 9:30 A.M. to 4:30 P.M. except some holidays. Tours of Glenmont begin hourly, 10 A.M. to 4 P.M., Monday through Saturday.

VIII

EMPIRE BUILDERS
AND LEADERS OF MEN

Soon after the Civil War, while writers, artists and inventors were producing a flood of created things, the country saw an explosive era of expansion and development in industry, transportation, mining, manufacture and finance that lasted well into the twentieth century. Many of the men who engineered and directed the expansion made great personal fortunes; some of them built opulent mansions and personal palaces.

During the same period other men rose to heights as master politicians and leaders of men and helped transform the nation through the impact of their leadership. The mansions of empire builders and the homes of political leaders were in many regions across the country. Newport, Rhode Island, became a fashionable resort of the very rich. Upper Fifth Avenue in New York City was lined with the ornate houses of millionaires. Other houses were at the center of great estates. A very limited selection of these houses, extending across the country and ranging widely in character, are described in this chapter. They include: two houses of the dynamic President of the United States, Theodore Roosevelt—his birthplace in the heart of New York City and a family estate on nearby Long Island; a Venetian palace overlooking a lagoon in Sarasota, Florida, built by John Ringling, the very rich and successful circus owner; an estate and rambling manor house in Hyde Park, New York, overlooking the Hudson River, birthplace and lifetime home of a great President of the United States, Franklin D. Roosevelt; a vast baronial estate near Asheville, North Carolina, built by the enlightened multimillionaire George W. Vanderbilt; the incredibly lavish and bizarre hilltop mansion and estate near San Simeon in California from which William Randolph Hearst ruled the nation's biggest publishing empire; and finally, in northern

California, overlooking Eureka, a grotesque and fascinating Victorian mansion built by a lumber baron named Carson.

Theodore Roosevelt Homes

By heritage and birth Theodore Roosevelt was a New Yorker, and through a long, dynamic life in public service, as writer, explorer, soldier and twenty-sixth President of the United States, New York remained his home. The two houses where he spent most of his life, his birthplace in the heart of New York City, and a hilltop family mansion on Long Island, called "Sagamore Hill," are both national historic sites and public shrines. Together, with vivid detail, they tell the life story of a truly great American.

BIRTHPLACE

Theodore Roosevelt was born on October 27, 1858, at 28 East Twentieth Street, New York City, child of a wealthy, patrician family. An ancestor, Claes Martenszan van Rosenvelt, had migrated to New Amsterdam in 1650.

Generations later, Theodore's father, Theodore, Sr., married a beautiful southern girl and brought her to New York to live in a four-story brownstone townhouse, in the heart of the then fashionable Madison Square district. There, four years later, Theodore was born. The house, typical of many in New York during the midyears of the nineteenth century, was the Roosevelt home for the next fifteen years.

For several years after young Teddy's birth he was sickly, plagued with asthma. But when he was about twelve years old, as an aid to his health, his father installed a well-equipped small gymnasium on the rear porch of the family home. Young Teddy doggedly worked out on the apparatus. It helped him turn the corner between poor health and vigor. Within a year the asthma had disappeared and Teddy was on his way to becoming a man of inexhaustible vitality and surging energy, qualities he retained throughout his life.

When Teddy was fifteen years old the family moved to a new district and a house at 6 West Fifty-seventh Street. The Roosevelt family continued to own the Twentieth Street house until 1896. Thereafter the Madison Square district slowly changed from a fashionable residential section to a business area, with most of the townhouses that once lined Twentieth Street replaced by commercial buildings. Fortunately the Roosevelt birthplace was not torn down and in 1919 it was acquired by the Women's Roosevelt Memorial Association, which later merged with the Theodore Roosevelt Association. The association raised money to preserve and restore Theodore Roosevelt's birthplace, along with the house adjoining it to the west, once the home of Theodore's Uncle Robert.

Careful restoration of the two houses has resulted in an almost perfect

In 1858, Theodore Roosevelt was born in this narrow brownstone town house in the heart of the then-fashionable Madison Square district of New York City. Now hemmed in by towering commercial buildings, the old house has become a national shrine. *Photograph: Courtesy National Park Service.*

The classically elegant
Victorian parlor was
remembered by Roosevelt as
"a room of much splendor."
*Photograph: Courtesy
National Park Service.*

Carefully restored, the room
where Theodore Roosevelt
was born now looks at it did
when he was a child. The
portrait is of his mother.
*Photograph: Courtesy
National Park Service.*

re-creation of a typical Victorian townhouse. Today it is seen almost exactly as it was during the years Theodore, Jr., lived there as a boy. Robert Roosevelt's house next door was converted into a small, fascinating museum filled with relics of Theodore Roosevelt's life: documents, pictures, trophies and gifts are arranged so that by strolling through the house visitors gain a vivid impression of the many-faceted Roosevelt career.

The living rooms and two bedrooms of the birthplace have been restored to the period of Teddy's youth, with much of the original furniture, pictures and draperies. Rooms of special interest include a handsome drawing room with a high ceiling, magnificent mirrors, crystal chandelier and blue satin draperies all displayed with the characteristic elegance of the period. Many years later, in writing about the house as he remembered it, Roosevelt said that for the children ". . . this was a room of much splendor . . . open for general use only on Sunday evening or on rare occasions when there were parties."

The front bedroom is now almost precisely as it was at Teddy's birth, with the original furniture and a charming portrait of Theodore's mother. A nursery adjoins and behind that is the open porch, equipped as young Teddy's health-restoring home gymnasium. A feature of the house was the arrangement of the yard at the back. Both houses (the birthplace and Uncle Robert's house) had wide porches overlooking adjoining yards and the gardens of the Robert Goelet estate fronting on Nineteenth Street. Because of the commercial character of the neighborhood now, no attempt has been made to restore the garden areas.

Not long after leaving the birthplace home Theodore, Jr., entered Harvard, graduating in 1880. The year of his graduation he married Alice Hathaway Lee, member of a distinguished Boston family, and returned to New York to attend Columbia Law School and dabble in politics, starting with a seat in the New York State Assembly.

SAGAMORE HILL HOME, OYSTER BAY, NEW YORK

Six months after his graduation from Harvard, Roosevelt acquired a tract at Cove Neck, just east of the village of Oyster Bay on Long Island's northern shore. He had known the land and come to love it as a boy when the family summered at Oyster Bay and young Teddy and his friends roamed the wooded hills to the east. He intended to build a family home on the hill, which he called "Sagamore" from old Sagamore Mohannis, chief of an Indian tribe who had signed away rights to the land two hundred years earlier.

Altogether Roosevelt bought 155 acres for $10,000 in cash and a $20,000 mortgage. Roosevelt kept ninety-five acres and sold the rest to his sister, Anna, and his mother's sister, Gracie. Though partially cultivated, the land was rugged and mostly wooded with splendid old trees, a perfect site for the home of a growing family.

Sagamore Hill, a rambling Victorian mansion set in spacious wooded grounds on Long Island, was the family home of Theodore Roosevelt throughout a long and vigorous life. *Photograph: Courtesy National Park Service.*

New York architects were engaged to design a house for a young man of substance who expected to have a large family. The plans called for a big, solidly built house to crown a hilltop. There would be wide porches, fireplaces everywhere (four on the first floor). The style was Victorian.

In writing about the plans Roosevelt gives some clues as to what he wanted: "I arranged . . . to get what I desired as far as my money permitted. . . . I wished a big piazza where we could sit in rocking chairs and watch the sunset; a library with a shallow bay window looking south; the parlor or drawing room occupying all the western end of the lower floor . . . big fireplaces for logs. . . ."

But before a contract could be signed Alice Roosevelt died in childbirth. The child lived and was named for her mother. Because Roosevelt decided that his new daughter must have a home, two weeks after his wife's death he signed a contract for the building of a twenty-two-room house. It would cost $16,975.

During the year the house was being built and for a period afterward Roosevelt fled to the badlands of South Dakota where he tried to blanket his grief with physical activity: running a cattle ranch, hunting, riding on a roundup. In the meantime his sister, Anna, moved into Sagamore Hill and took care of baby Alice there. But the next year, 1886, Roosevelt was persuaded to return to New York to run for mayor. He lost, but Sagamore Hill became his home, and remained the house to which he always returned during the rest of his remarkable life. An interlude that helped convert the house to the family home planned was his marriage in London to a childhood friend, Edith Kermit Carow, who became the mother of a growing family, and Sagamore Hill one of the most celebrated homes of America. Statesmen, politicians, writers, big-game hunters and polo players flocked to it. Sagamore Hill became a focal point of local and national politics, reflecting every facet of an increasingly important career in public service that included such posts as member of the United States Civil Service Commission, president of the New York City's Police Board, Assistant Secretary of the Navy, lieutenant colonel of the Rough Riders regiment in the Spanish-American War, governor of New York, Vice-President of the United States and, finally, upon the assassination of President McKinley on September 14, 1901, President of the United States.

In summer, from 1901 to 1909, Sagamore Hill was the center of the day-to-day administration of the country's affairs, a setting for events of both national and international interest. Important visitors were received and entertained from all over the world. It was there, in the library of Sagamore Hill, that Roosevelt separately met the envoys of warring Russia and Japan and brought them face to face in a decisive step to conclude the 1905 Treaty of Portsmouth, New Hampshire.

After leaving the White House, Sagamore Hill became a year-round home, to which Roosevelt always returned from trips including big game hunting in Africa, exploring in the jungles of Brazil, a visit to the German Kaiser and lecturing at Oxford and at the Sorbonne in Paris. The historic house was campaign headquarters for the ill-fated Bull Moose campaign of

1912, in which Roosevelt as head of a new Independent party opposed President Taft for reelection.

Over the years Sagamore Hill gathered a huge and fascinating collection of furniture, trophies, souvenirs, historic documents, cartoons, photographs, guns, flags and books, reflecting wide-ranging interests and achievements. Most of them are at Sagamore Hill now, displayed as they were when Theodore Roosevelt died in 1919.

Following his death Edith Roosevelt continued to live at Sagamore Hill until her death in 1949 at the age of eighty-seven. Thereafter public interest made the house first a local then a national shrine, and finally a national historic site maintained and exhibited by the National Park Service.

Many thousands of fascinated visitors flock to the house every year to roam through it and wander over the handsome grounds. They find the estate from the historic village of Oyster Bay by following Cove Neck Road to the crest of the hill and tip of the rugged peninsula where it stands overlooking Cold Spring Harbor on the east, Oyster Bay Harbor on the west.

Visitors enter across the piazza into a spacious central hall, and immediately enter the life of Theodore Roosevelt. The hall, running through the house, gives a glimpse of what is to come: animal trophies on the walls, furniture and paintings acquired through Roosevelt's life. Though all rooms of the house open to the public are of interest to visitors, some are more fascinating than others. Furnishings are original Roosevelt pieces, and in every room are things that were used and loved by the family. Crowded bookshelves reveal the wide range of Roosevelt's interests; many books he wrote himself.

Of special interest is the library, actually Roosevelt's study or private office. It probably saw the beginning of more important events during Roosevelt's terms as President than any other place except the Oval Room of the White House. It is cluttered with family portraits, the inevitable trophy heads and skins, crammed bookcases, comfortable but nondescript Victorian furniture.

Other lower-floor rooms include the dining room, filled with ornate and massive Italian furniture bought in Florence on the Roosevelt honeymoon, and the bright and cheerful drawing room, Mrs. Roosevelt's special room.

Stunning climax to any visit to Sagamore Hill is the splendid North, or Trophy, Room. Added in 1904 to contain the growing collection of Roosevelt trophies and historic possessions, it is a huge, high-ceilinged room, thirty feet by forty feet. It was designed by C. Grant La Farge, a Roosevelt friend, and is one of the few rooms in the house not in the Victorian mood. The room glows with the luminous tones of polished woods, mahogany walls, black walnut columns, American cypress in the ceiling beams. It is crammed with trophies of hunting expeditions: skins, elephant tusks, mounted heads. There are flags: the President's, a regimental flag of the Rough Riders and a poignant flag from the grave of Quentin Roosevelt, killed in World War I. Every piece of furniture has a special association with Roosevelt. Some pieces are gifts from the great of the world, others specially designed for the room or brought from the White House. There are historic

paintings, including a famous one of Roosevelt, and a wealth of fascinating odds and ends. Bookshelves are filled with special treasures.

Upstairs rooms are intimate family rooms, each with special association for the Roosevelt family. They range from President and Mrs. Roosevelt's bedroom with its vast, incredibly ornate bed that won a prize at the 1876 Philadelphia Exposition, to the family nursery, and include a remarkable bathroom, the only one in the house, with an enormous heavy porcelain tub.

The third floor has a special room, the Gun Room, where Roosevelt kept his collection of rifles and shotguns and where he sometimes entertained special visitors, or retired to write or work.

Though some visitors pay little attention to the wide piazza extending along the southern and western sides of the house, it was a very important area when Sagamore Hill was the Roosevelt family home. Strewn with rocking chairs and tables it was a much-used family area. Of it Roosevelt wrote, "The big piazza is for the still, hot afternoons of summer." From it at night, he wrote, you could rock and "watch the lights of the tall Fall River boats as they steam steadily by."

For some, especially nature lovers, the extensive grounds are a delight. Many of the big, splendid trees were planted by Roosevelt or some member of the family. Some are rare species of historic interest, gifts to the estate from friends.

A footnote to Sagamore Hill is Theodore Roosevelt's grave at the heart of a bird sanctuary, about a mile east of the village of Oyster Bay and overlooking the quiet waters of Oyster Bay Harbor.

Biltmore House, George W. Vanderbilt Home, Asheville, North Carolina

The spectacular North, or Trophy, Room of Theodore Roosevelt's Sagamore Hill home is crammed with hunting trophies, hundreds of relics and souvenirs of his long and remarkable life. *Photograph: Courtesy National Park Service.*

About 1885 George W. Vanderbilt, grandson of Commodore Cornelius Vanderbilt and one of the richest men in America, began looking for a site where he might build a repository for his growing collection of art treasures. He finally chose an area near Asheville, North Carolina, a region of farms, woodlands and forested mountains. There in 1888 he began to buy land that eventually amounted to nearly 200,000 acres. At the heart of his new land he planned to build the finest country house in America.

To design his house he selected a friend, Richard Morris Hunt, one of the country's leading architects and a special authority on Vanderbilt's favorite architectural period, the French Renaissance. To lay out his estate, both the vast forest areas and the extensive gardens that would surround the house, he selected the country's leading landscape architect best known for the development of Central Park in New York City, Frederick Law Olmsted.

Together Vanderbilt and Hunt decided on a château-type mansion, with elements and details suggested by the classic château of the Loire Valley in France, particularly the chateau at Blois. The area was scoured for workers,

and craftsmen with special skills were brought from many parts of this country and Europe to cut, fit and carve the Indiana limestone that would be the main material for the great house. More than a thousand workers and craftsmen were engaged at the site for about five years to complete the splendid 250-room house. While it was under construction Vanderbilt roamed Europe for tapestries, statuary, furniture, paintings and art treasures to grace the ornate and opulent rooms. The house, fully furnished with the classic elegance of the Renaissance, was formally opened with a Christmas party in 1895. For a number of years after that it was the official home of Mr. Vanderbilt and his wife, Edith Stuyvesant Dresser, direct descendant of New York's (Nieuw Amsterdam's) Dutch governor Peter Stuyvesant. The name of the house, "Biltmore," was a contrived combination of Dutch, "Bildt"—the Dutch town that was the ancestral Vanderbilt home (van der Bildt)—and an old English word "more," meaning high, rolling, upland country.

While the house was being built the development of the enormous mountain estate was proceeding under the direction of Gifford Pinchot, a pioneer in forest development who was recommended by Olmsted. On the estate Pinchot soon demonstrated that scientific forest management was both practical and profitable, and established the first forestry school in the United States there.

The grounds immediately surrounding the great house were developed under Olmsted's direction into a series of superb garden areas, in part resembling the gardens of Vaux Le Vicomte in France, but with less formal special gardens including a vast rose garden, and the largest azalea garden in the country.

During his lifetime Vanderbilt maintained Biltmore House as his private residence. It was not open to the public. When he died in 1914, his daughter, Cornelia, who had married John Francis Amherst Cecil, became the mistress of Biltmore House. Soon after Vanderbilt's death Mrs. Cecil deeded a large share of the huge estate to the United States government as the nucleus of Pisgah National Forest, an area that included Pisgah Peak, first national forest to be created in the East.

In 1930, sixteen years after the death of Mr. Vanderbilt, Mr. and Mrs. Cecil were persuaded to open Biltmore House and gardens to the public. Since then the great house with its superb gardens has been seen by thousands of visitors, particularly in the spring and summer when the floral splendors of the grounds and gardens are at their peak.

Visitors approach the house through lodge gates of Biltmore Village, then follow a winding approach road for three miles through plantings of pine, hemlock and hardwoods, accented by flowering mountain shrubs. The

Patterned on the opulent French Château at Blois, Biltmore House, near Asheville, North Carolina, was built by George W. Vanderbilt who wanted the "finest country home in America." *Photograph: Courtesy North Carolina Department of Conservation.*

▶

At the heart of a 200,000-acre forested estate, Biltmore House is surrounded by wide lawns and splendid gardened areas. *Photograph: Courtesy North Carolina Department of Conservation.*

road sweeps up to the main entrance centered in a façade that suggests the great Château at Blois, in the Loire Valley of France, a favorite residence of French kings. The interior of the house, carrying out the Renaissance traditions of France, England, Spain, Italy, Holland and Germany with lavish elegance, is generally recognized as having the most complete and finest collection of Renaissance treasures—furniture, painting, tapestry and decorative details—outside of museums.

Most important rooms of the house are open to the public, and can be viewed on tours led by experienced guides. All rooms visited are remarkable in one way or another; some are spectacular.

Special details and rooms of high interest include the grand staircase, a copy of one at the Château de Blois, winding around one of the world's largest wrought-iron chandeliers. Off the main entrance is the famed Palm Court, an interior garden area filled at all times with masses of flowers, grouped around a charming fountain, from the estate gardens. Most extraordinary room in the mansion is the banquet hall, suggesting baronial great halls of medieval palaces, with an arched ceiling rising seventy-five feet above a room that measured 72 by 42 feet. A huge triple fireplace at one end faces a towering pipe organ behind a gallery at the other. Along the walls are carved Gothic thrones between rare Flemish tapestries. From the lofty ceiling hang enormous circular chandeliers, and around the walls, high above the tremendous banquet table, are trophy heads and flags.

Other notable rooms include the intimate oak drawing room, paneled with Norwegian oak, walls lined with portraits and photographs of members of the Vanderbilt family; a stunning high-ceilinged library, paneled in walnut, shelves filled with more than twenty thousand books, many of them rare, some unique treasures. A fascinating feature of the room is an elegant spiral staircase leading to a book-lined gallery. A lavishly appointed oak sitting room suggests one of the great rooms of a Tudor manor house in England.

Most visitors during spring, summer and autumn find the remarkable gardens of the estate worth exploring, for they are matched by no other domestic gardens in the country. They include a formal terrace with some of the country's finest boxwood, an Italian garden with three formal pools, a remarkable mixed hedge of holly and hemlock. A four-acre walled garden has been called the "finest English garden in America." A vast rose garden has more than five thousand plants. The azalea garden, generally regarded as the finest in the world, has every known example of domestic or exotic as well as rare magnolias and some of the most splendid evergreens in North America. A final note is a bass pond fed by a stream tumbling over a waterfall, overhung by the largest cypress tree in cultivation in the country.

The estate's extensive conservatory and associated greenhouses, providing year-round flowers for the huge house and plantings for all the gardens, are open to visitors. Collateral exhibits include a four-thousand-acre dairy farm with one of the finest and largest dairy herds in the world, and more than ten thousand acres of superbly maintained forest land.

Sweeping up in a graceful spiral, the grand stairway, a copy of one at the Château Blois, winds around one of the world's largest wrought-iron chandeliers. *Photograph: Courtesy North Carolina Department of Conservation.*

Few sleeping rooms anywhere
are larger and more ornate
than the vast master bedroom,
fit for the sleep of a Tudor
King. *Photograph: Courtesy
North Carolina Department
of Commerce.*

Most remarkable and splendid
room of Biltmore House is the
banquet hall, suggesting the
baronial great hall of a
medieval palace. *Photograph:
Courtesy North Carolina
Department of Commerce.*

Ca' d' Zan, John Ringling Home, Sarasota, Florida

Owning and operating a circus is not the usual way to become rich. More circus owners have gone bankrupt than have acquired wealth. A spectacular exception was John Ringling, who became king of the circus world, chief owner and manager of a merger of the nation's biggest circuses, Ringling Brothers and Barnum and Bailey. He was one of the country's richest men, with large interests in other fields such as oil, mining, ranching and real estate.

As an expression of his wealth and taste, John Ringling, during the flamboyant mid-twenties, decided to build a splendid palace as his home. The site chosen was Sarasota, Florida, his favorite city, that would become the winter home of his gigantic circus. There, over a period of several years, Ringling built an opulent mansion of unrivaled magnificence. It was called "Ca' d' Zan," which translates from a Venetian dialect to "the House of John." But more responsible for it than John Ringling himself was his wife, Mabel, who made the remarkable plans for its building and was a prime mover in collecting the vast assortment of ornate art and furnishings that would fill the palace.

On their many trips abroad to find circus talent John and Mabel Ringling fell in love with the colorful Renaissance magnificence of Venice. They wanted their home in Florida to be like a Venetian palazzo, but no ordinary one. It was to combine and resemble as much as possible two of Mabel Ringling's favorite buildings, the sumptuous Venetian Gothic Doge's Palace overlooking the Grand Canal of Venice and Madison Square Garden in New York City, built in association with Tex Rickard and owned by John Ringling. The site would be a thirty-seven-acre tract fronting Sarasota Bay, which, while not exactly the Grand Canal of Venice, promised a tropical waterfront of potential beauty.

Mabel Ringling's specifications for the Florida palace gave massive headaches to architectural associates engaged to carry out the plans, which were finally modified with concessions for design by architect Dwight James Baum into a fabulous expression of luxury, elegance and grandeur in a setting of beguiling loveliness. At a time when other men who had made fortunes were engaging the architect Addison Misner to build Spanish palaces and castles in Florida, the Ringling dwelling was unique. The mansion itself cost about $1 million. Half again that sum went into the exotic gardens and another half million bought furnishings and art work that filled the house.

The Ringling story is an American classic in the Horatio Alger pattern. There was nothing in his early life as the member of a large family of modest circumstances to suggest that John, youngest of seven brothers would become the owner of the world's greatest aggregation of entertainment talent.

John Ringling was born in 1866 at Baraboo, Wisconsin, a village a few miles northwest of Madison. His father, a harness maker, had migrated to America from Germany some years earlier and changed his name from Rungeling to Ringling. Like many Germans the family loved music. John and his brothers were fascinated by little circuses that callioped through the villages of Wisconsin in the summer months. John was only sixteen when the brothers decided to go into the entertainment field. In 1882 they launched the Classic and Comic Concert Company, in which two brothers danced while the others played musical instruments. Their first touring season netted $300. Two years later they started a small circus that traveled by wagon and exhibited a trained horse and a dancing bear. John was the clown, as well as the advance agent in charge of business arrangements. He must have been good at the job because the Ringling circus prospered. By 1888 the Ringling brothers added an elephant and by 1900 they had one of the largest shows in the country, steadily buying out smaller shows until in 1919 the Ringling circus absorbed the mighty Barnum and Bailey show and became in the argot of circus life "the big one"—the largest, most splendid and successful circus in the world—and John, its principal owner and manager.

In the meantime John and Mabel Ringling had discovered Sarasota, Florida. In 1912, the year after John's first visit to Sarasota, they bought a tract on the north edge of the town, overlooking Sarasota Bay, built a sea-wall and began landscaping, while living several months each year in a modest house that stood on the land. Slowly plans for Ca' d' Zan matured. The Ringlings roamed Europe, buying vast assortments of material for the new house and art treasures to fill it. In Barcelona John Ringling found a bargain in used red roof tiles and bought two shiploads of them, enough for his own house and several houses of his Sarasota neighbors. Other things acquired included great quantities of Venetian glass in shades of purple, rose, amethyst, green and straw and special stonelike onyx from Mexico. From the United States came such accessories as a great glass chandelier from the then being demolished Waldorf Astoria in New York, pecky cypress from Florida for ceiling beams, leaded glass windows from a famous St. Louis barroom. A special contribution from Mabel Ringling's beloved Venice was an authentic gondola to be tethered to a tiny island in the bay. But a storm washed away the island and sank the gondola. Bronze ornaments from it are among the decorative oddities in the mansion today.

▷
Wealthy from circus profits, John Ringling built Ca' d' Zan, "the house of John," on the edge of a Florida lagoon. It was designed to resemble a Venetian palace. *Photograph: Courtesy Ringling Museum.*

Another view of Ca' d' Zan, on the
edge of a Florida lagoon.

When the splendid, exotically ornate mansion was finished at last, the
main house extended two hundred feet along the bay. A square tower rose
more than sixty feet above the main entrance. Inside the palazzo, more than
thirty rooms spread out from a huge great hall extending up two stories.

Visitors today see the house as it was when lived in by John and Mabel
Ringling. It is crowded with possessions, paintings, tapestries and furnishings that reflect their tastes and tell the story of John Ringling's robust and
successful life. The Ringling tastes, neither subdued nor conservative, included sumptuous reproductions of historic styles of the past, French Gothic
and French and Italian Renaissance. Much of the furniture is excessively
gilded and carved, often heavy. Precious wood inlays are everywhere.
Throughout the house, but particularly in the great hall, there is a wealth
of intricate and delicate hand-wrought iron work. Many wall areas are
covered with Flemish and English tapestries of mythological and religious
subjects.

Though the whole house is remarkable as now maintained and displayed by the state of Florida, some rooms are notable. These include the

222

Largest room in the Ringling
mansion is the two-story,
balconied great hall, typically
Italianate in design and set
with ornate appointments.
*Photograph: Courtesy
Ringling Museum.*

two-story great hall opening from the foyer, a typically Italianate room, largest in the palace and ornate and splendid in its appointments; the huge ballroom with a golden magnificence, an intricate coffered ceiling to which Willy Pogany contributed frescoes showing dances from all the world; it is a far cry from the bar lounge which is typical of St. Louis at the turn of the century and which has accessories and decor brought from the famous Winter Palace Restaurant, one of John Ringling's favorites. John Ringling's huge bedroom sets a different note: French Empire, with furniture of rosewood encrusted with gilt. Visitors to the room can peek into a vast closet where John Ringling's wardrobe of dozens of suits, coats and figured silk ties still hangs. Even more overwhelming is the regal luxury of Ringling's bathroom, with walls of Siena marble and an enormous tub carved from a huge block of the same stone. Fixtures are gold-plated. The most practical feature of the room is the barber chair. Ringling's office is a highly personal room, with walls and cabinets crowded with souvenirs of his colorful life and relics of the circus. Pictures include portraits of all his brothers; a revolving bookcase has books he especially liked, and on the big square desk is a silver telephone, a gift from the Vatican at Rome. One of the most delightful rooms is a third-floor gaming room reached by a spiral stairway. It has the excitement and color of a Venetian festival, with a ceiling mural done by Pogany where a swirling fantasy of dance and carnival includes portraits of John and Mabel Ringling.

John Ringling's bedroom is big and opulent, the furniture French Empire encrusted with gilt. *Photograph: Courtesy Ringling Museum.*

▷

Decorated with the color of a Venetian festival, most delightful room in the Ringling mansion is the attic fun room, with a ceiling mural a swirling fantasy of dance and carnival. *Photograph: Courtesy Ringling Museum.*

Visitors who take the trouble to explore the grounds are amply rewarded in discovering immaculately manicured acres set with the most exotically beautiful of Florida's trees, shrubbery and flowers including palms, banyan, live oak, hibiscus, often seen among riotously blooming bougainvillaea, oleander and poinsettia. There are hundreds of sculptured figures from Venice including jaunty little cupids, or *putti*, lining driveways.

John and Mabel Ringling had only three years together in their Venetian palazzo. In 1929 came disaster and tragedy. In that year Mabel Ringling died, the stock market crashed and the Depression followed, which was calamitous for John. New York bankers took over management of the circus, leaving Ringling a lonely and broken man. He died in 1936 at the age of seventy but not before a start had been made to fulfill two other dreams associated with his palace home: the establishment of the Ringling Museum, the palatial baroque gallery that would house his vast collection of art; and the unique Circus Museum, crowded with relics of circuses from all ages, including Ringling's own "Greatest Show on Earth." Both are on the property of Ca' d' Zan.

Franklin D. Roosevelt Birthplace, Hyde Park, New York

Franklin D. Roosevelt, thirty-second President of the United States, was born on his father's estate near Hyde Park, New York, on January 30, 1882, and considered it his home the rest of his life. This fact makes the celebrated Roosevelt birthplace on the east bank of the Hudson River almost unique among historic houses. Few other dwellings owe their fame to lifetime residence by the man whose achievements give them historic interest.

Throughout Roosevelt's extraordinary life he always came back to the Hyde Park estate to live and rest whenever he could—from the White House, from Campobello Island, from Warm Springs, Georgia, from abroad. With his death Hyde Park became a national historic site. Visitors see the big, rambling manor house filled with intimate and revealing Roosevelt possessions overlooking a splendid vista of the Hudson River that Roosevelt loved. They see Roosevelt's grave and the grave of his wife, Eleanor, in the family rose garden and nearby the big Roosevelt library and museum.

The Hudson River Valley was a familiar region for several generations of Roosevelt ancestors. The first Roosevelts in the New World came from Holland in the early years of the seventeenth century and like other Dutch families acquired extensive lands and considerable wealth, to become members of the patrician Hudson River aristocracy.

Franklin Roosevelt's father, James Roosevelt, had bought the land of the family estate, together with a house that stood on it, in 1867. The land amounted to about two hundred acres of partially wooded rolling hills that sloped down to the Hudson River. The house standing at the crest of the

Starting as a modest farmhouse, the birthplace and lifetime home of Franklin Roosevelt grew into a rambling Georgian mansion that has become a national shrine. Photograph: Courtesy National Park Service.

hills didn't amount to much, a two-story clapboard frame house built in 1826. Almost at once Roosevelt's father began changing and extending the house, a process that continued for more than forty years. By the time Franklin Roosevelt was born in 1882 it had increased substantially in size, acquired a low, square tower, wide porches and a distinctly Victorian aspect.

By 1915, when Roosevelt was Assistant Secretary of the Navy, changes and extensions had brought the big house to its present aspect, a modified Georgian mansion. At either end a two-story wing had been built, extending over front and back, framing a wide terrace on the front, giving the house an H-shape plan. In addition to the wide front terrace there were porches at each end and at the rear overlooking the Hudson River. A traditional widow's walk linked twin chimneys. The interior contained more than thirty rooms, including seven bathrooms and seven fireplaces, with nine rooms in the north wing reserved for servants. The family rooms ranged from a huge living room and library, filling all of the lower floor of the south wing with twin fireplaces and two big bay windows, to a small octagonal smoking room off the dining room. Forty-eight years of development and change since James Roosevelt acquired the house converted a simple country house into an extensive mansion. Together with its handsomely landscaped grounds, it was a true manor house in the best Hudson River tradition.

In the meantime Roosevelt had launched himself on a public career almost unparalleled in American history. Graduating from Harvard in 1904 he married a distant cousin, Eleanor Roosevelt, in 1905, and later attended Columbia University Law School. Thereafter, as the squire of Hyde Park, he was successively state senator from the district of his residence, Assistant Secretary of the Navy and governor of New York. He emerged on the national political scene with a notable speech nominating Alfred E. Smith for the Presidency. The speech became a springboard for Roosevelt's own presidential aspirations. In 1932, at the depth of a national depression, in an atmosphere of fear and panic, he defeated Herbert Hoover for the Presidency of the United States.

His Presidency ushered in an era of crisis and change, which saw more adjustments in the pattern of national life than had ever occurred before. The threat of World War II became a reality, and Roosevelt, Commander-in-Chief of the greatest military force ever assembled, became a world leader. Throughout the years of his Presidency the Hyde Park house was often his headquarters. From it the President made many of the informal speeches and fireside chats for which he became famous. To Hyde Park flocked a procession of political and military leaders, representatives of foreign governments and business executives.

But throughout the years the Hyde Park estate was very much a family home. The Roosevelt children were all born and grew up there. Roosevelt's mother, Sara Delano, made it her home after the death of her husband. The house is filled, some rooms cluttered, with a thousand and one souvenirs of family life. There are playthings of the children, pictures of generations of

Model of the famed Grecian statue *Winged Victory*, one of many gifts made to Franklin Roosevelt, dominates the east portico of the huge family room. *Photograph: Courtesy National Park Service.*

Roosevelts, gifts sent to Roosevelt from all over the world, dozens of naval prints, even the chair used by Fala, the President's favorite Scottie, along with the dog's leash and blanket. There is little in the house to suggest the hand of an interior decorator, little coordinated elegance, but much to reveal that it was a comfortable, thoroughly lived-in mansion.

The National Park Service administers the estate, and informed guides lead groups through the house, where most of the family rooms are on exhibit. Such a visit evokes a vivid, often poignant understanding of President Roosevelt and his family, their habits, interests, hobbies, friends, travels and adventures. Rooms of special interest include the spacious living room and library where portraits of Roosevelt's ancestors hang above both fire-

places. The President's favorite leather chair is there, and also the family's favorite portrait of him.

Most colorful room in the house is the Dresden, or Drawing, Room with bright chintz draperies and upholstered furniture covered with the same material and an ornate marble mantel with a Dresden clock and matching chandeliers. Upstairs rooms include a suite filling the wing above the living room, with a sitting room and two bedrooms, one of which, a big room in the corner with a fireplace, was President's Roosevelt's. The walls are hung with family portraits and naval prints, and the room is still maintained as it was when the President left it in March, 1945, to go to Warm Springs, Georgia, where he died.

For generations Roosevelt estates, both in this country and Holland, had featured rose gardens. Roosevelt means "field of roses," and three roses on a shield are part of the family cost of arms. The President's tomb is a Vermont marble block, designed from plans President Roosevelt himself drew. Accessory buildings on the extensive grounds include a large greenhouse, a stable where family carriages are maintained with trophies and ribbons won by Roosevelt horses and with pictures and harness.

The very big Roosevelt library and museum is some distance from the family mansion and is separately administered under the direction of the Archivist of the United States. Thousands of books, official and personal papers relating to the period of Roosevelt's Presidency are housed there, along with a collection of pictures, ship models, art objects, and souvenirs of that period.

The Roosevelt home is easily reached. The estate entrance is two miles south of the village of Hyde Park and four miles north of the city of Poughkeepsie, on the New York–Albany Post Road, US 9. A convenient route from New York City would be via the Henry Hudson Parkway, Saw Mill River Parkway and Taconic State Parkway taking US 44 from the Taconic west into Poughkeepsie to US 9. The estate is open to visitors daily, except Christmas Day, from 9 A.M. to 5:30 P.M. Hours for visiting the library and museum are slightly different.

The Enchanted Hill, William Randolph Hearst Home, San Simeon, California

Brightly flowered chintz coverings and matching draperies make the drawing room the gayest room in the Hyde Park mansion. *Photograph: Courtesy National Park Service.*

Some years ago motorists traveling California's spectacular coastal highway between Morro Bay and Carmel occasionally stopped at a village called San Simeon where an enterprising promotor maintained a coin-in-the-slot telescope. On a clear day, by focusing it up and east, they could see the tops of twin ivory towers about five miles away. The towers were part of the Hearst castle, and San Simeon was as close as ordinary people could get to the fabulous mansion, since only guests of William Randolph Hearst en-

The Neptune pool at the Hearst mountaintop estate, flanked by Greek and Roman temples, is one of the largest and most beautiful private swimming pools. The pool is faced with white marble and set with green marble mosaics. *Photograph: Courtesy California Division of Parks.*

◄

Ornate and splendid, the twin towers of William Randolph Hearst's incredible mansion, La Casa Grande, at San Simeon, California, soar above the exotic Spanish Renaissance façade of the great house. *Photograph: Courtesy California Division of Parks.*

joyed a closer look. Hearst, the very wealthy publishing tycoon, called his hilltop estate high in the Santa Lucia Mountains, "La Cuesta Encantado," or "The Enchanted Hill." At the time California was rife with rumors about the Hearst mountaintop home: reports of how it had been built, what it was and what it contained. It was said that exotic animals roamed the mountain slopes between the mansion and the sea; that the estate included a private zoo and a vast marble swimming pool framed by Greek and Roman temples; that interior rooms of the mansion were crowded with incredible treasures of art and furnishings brought to California by persuasive Hearst dollars from palaces, castles, churches, museums, monasteries, châteaux and temples of Spain, France, Italy, Greece, and England.

From time to time the rumors were confirmed and amplified by reports from guests, ranging from world leaders to movie starlets, who told of a manner of living on top of The Enchanted Hill more sumptuous than that of a medieval monarch.

233

But in 1958, seven years after Hearst's death, La Cuesta Encantado stopped being a place of mystery and legend. In that year Hearst heirs gave the mansion to the state of California as a memorial to Hearst and Hearst's mother, Phoebe Apperson Hearst. Since then millions of incredulous visitors have been bussed up the hill over a five-mile approach highway, usually glimpsing en route strange animals roaming among the trees. At the crest of the mountain they emerge into sunlight and a dazzling prospect of one of the most ornately splendid mansions in the world, La Casa Grande, with twin Spanish towers rising 137 feet. All around the central mansion are terraces and gardens, a setting for smaller guest mansions, and two incredible swimming pools. Inside the mansion itself they see great chambers and lofty halls crowded with an unbelievable collection of rare paintings, sculpture, furniture and tapestries.

The story of William Randolph Hearst and his Enchanted Hill begins with his father, George Hearst, who, fresh from a midwestern college where he studied geology and engineering, trekked to California in 1850 in time to cash in on the gold rush. He did so with rewarding results—gold and silver strikes in California, Nevada and later in Mexico. By the time his son, William Randolph, was born in 1863 George Hearst was a very rich man and was beginning to acquire ranch lands. Before William Randolph returned from two years in Harvard at the age of twenty-four his father had become a United States Senator, and owned several hundred thousand acres of former Spanish ranch land as well as the then moribund newspaper the San Francisco *Examiner*. Both the newspaper and the ranch land would be crucial in young Hearst's future life.

Filled with ideas of what a newspaper should be William Randolph persuaded his father to give him the San Francisco *Examiner*. Then, backed by his father's wealth and using the flamboyant methods always character-istic of him, he went on to make the *Examiner* profitable. Using the Cali-fornia paper as a springboard into national journalism he built a publishing empire that at one time included thirty newspapers, fifteen magazines and six radio stations. As his fame and fortune increased Hearst began to find diversion in family picnics at the crest of his favorite mountain which the family called Camp Hill. It was part of the Piedre Blanca (white stone) Ranch, one of three Hearst-owned, former Spanish ranches stretching fifty miles along the Pacific Ocean and extending deep into wooded mountains, a vast rugged tract of 240,000 acres. The family picnic grounds were five miles east of the former whaling village of San Simeon, and the hill crest itself was sixteen hundred feet above the sea.

In 1919, when Hearst was fifty-three, he decided to make the mountain-top a site for a new home, though he already owned palatial houses in both New York and San Francisco. He wanted a place where he could exhibit a vast collection of art he had been acquiring in Europe. To help him he engaged Julia Morgan, a distinguished California architect, whose skills as a designer complimented Hearst's flair for the exotic. Together they selected building styles appropriate to the bright sun of southern California, chiefly

Mediterranean Renaissance and in particular the ornate baroque style of Spain.

With unlimited resources available work proceeded rapidly. Soon San Simeon's little harbor was filled with ships loaded with construction materials—tiles and marbles brought from abroad, steel, cement and timber. Other ships brought part of Hearst's vast collection of art. Everything was hauled up the hill. Water was piped from springs five miles away and the barren soil of the hilltop was replaced with rich soil where exotic plants and trees from all over the world would feel at home. While the gardens were being developed, the work of building went on. First completed were three luxurious guest houses on three sides of the hill crest. Each guest house was a palatial mansion in its own right; together they contained forty-six guest rooms. They were fitting satellites for the mansion that would crown the crest. Begun in 1922 La Casa Grande was still unfinished at the time of Hearst's death in 1951, but it had grown to a huge mansion of one hundred rooms, including thirty-nine bedrooms, thirty-one bathrooms, fourteen sitting rooms, a kitchen, movie theater, two libraries, a billiard room, lofty dining hall, or refectory, an assembly hall and others. Most of the rooms were vast in size, and magnificent with rare tiles, precious woods, Gothic and Renaissance tapestries, fine wood carving, huge French and Italian mantels, carved ceilings, Persian rugs and Roman mosaics.

But all the art treasures are not inside the mansion. Scattered over several acres of grounds at different levels and along wide promenades are marble statuary, well heads, sarcophagi, fountains and ornate stairways and terraces. Greek and Roman temple façades and Etruscan-style colonnades flank the 104-foot-long Neptune pool of white marble patterned with antique green marble mosaics. Another building that houses an indoor Roman pool is so large that two tennis courts are built on the roof. The walls of this building are lined with brilliant Venetian glass and gold tile. The more than one hundred acres of grounds immediately surrounding the mansion and complex of associated buildings include a mile-long pergola with espaliered fruit trees and grape vines. Among exotic trees from all over the world are forty Italian cypress, and equally exotic animals roamed among them during Hearst's day—zebra, tahr goats, aoudad (Barbary sheep). Some of their descendants are still there, and can be seen from the road that climbs to the hill crest.

But though visitors are fascinated by exterior features of The Enchanted Hill, they are awed by the lavish splendor of interior rooms; an assembly room, eighty-four feet long, thirty-five feet wide, twenty-three feet high; Hearst's favorite room, the refectory, with a lofty carved ceiling and priceless tapestries on the walls, where guests dined in regal pomp under gay heraldic banners of noble Italian families; two libraries, a main library with more than five thousand volumes, and a Gothic library, part of Hearst's personal suite; the celestial suite high in the two towers, under twin carillons; the Doge's suite, Venetian in style with a balcony copied from the Doge's Palace at Venice. There is a movie theater with nightly

showings for Hearst's guests who watched the screen from fifty luxurious loge seats. Everywhere throughout the mansion parts of the enormous Hearst art collection are displayed. It has been estimated that Hearst spent an average of one million dollars every year for fifty years on his collection and in the construction of La Casa Grande and its associated elements.

Though visiting the San Simeon estate can be easily arranged, the popularity of tours offered make it necessary to secure reservations well in advance. Three separate tours are available, each exhibiting different areas of the mansion and grounds. The mansion is maintained as the Hearst–San Simeon state historical monument, managed and exhibited by the Division of Parks and Recreation, Sacramento, California, through which reservations can be made by mail. Entrance to the estate is at San Simeon on California Highway 1, thirty miles north of Morro Bay, 191 miles south of Monterey. It is open to visitors every day, with each tour two hours long.

Carson Mansion, Eureka, California

Beginning a few miles north of San Francisco and extending to the Oregon border are forest giants called redwoods. Among the tallest and most beautiful trees in the world as well as the oldest, redwoods occur in majestic groves where sounds are muted and light has a cathedral-like quality. In recent years strenuous national and regional efforts have been made to protect the redwood trees, with the result that many groves are now within the limits of national and state forests.

But a hundred years ago, long before despoiling the land carried a stigma, few were concerned with guarding the redwood groves and a small army of forest vandals was busy felling the enormous trees and converting their splendid wood into timber. Some who did so became rich. One of the richest was William Carson who had first come to California from New Jersey in 1850 to dig for gold. He found gold and established a claim in the wild and beautiful Trinity River country just east of the village of Eureka, a coastal town in the heart of a district where there were (and still are) many groves of giant redwood trees. Carson thought felling the great trees a better idea than grubbing for gold, since he knew that the world needed lumber probably more than it needed gold. He organized crews of lumberjacks and sent them into redwood groves to chop down as many trees as possible. The enormous size of the trees created all sorts of problems. Often cutting down a single tree required the labor of a dozen men working with saws and axes on platforms high above the ground. Getting the fallen monarchs out of the forest and dragging them to sawmills was an even bigger problem. It was solved in part by the ingenuity of a Carson associate, John Dolbeer, who invented a single-cylinder side spool donkey engine that revolutionized logging.

In a few years Carson and Dolbeer had four huge lumber mills in and near Eureka, owned vast tracts of timber land with many redwood groves,

William Randolph Hearst's favorite room was the refectory, a large and lofty room, festooned with Italian heraldic banners, where a small army of guests might dine in regal pomp between walls covered with rare tapestries. *Photograph: Courtesy California Division of Parks.*

and operated a fleet of lumber schooners that carried their timber all over the world. By 1880 Carson was one of the richest men in northern California. He was renowned regionally, easily Eureka's first citizen and a genuine lumber king. But he didn't live like a lumber king. His home was a modest cottage high on a bluff overlooking the village of Eureka. From his windows he could see the smoke billowing from the high stacks of his several lumber mills and hear the whine of the big saws slicing the redwood trees into useful timber.

Carson was proud of his achievement and decided that his status deserved a dwelling that might be judged a suitable monument to him—a Carson Mansion. With simple logic he decided that his planned mansion should be built of redwood. The decision had more to it than sentiment. Redwood, then as now, is regarded as one of the finest building woods, clear grained, vermin-proof, almost fireproof and moisture resistant.

So in 1884 Carson hired more than one hundred carpenters and craftsmen to help build his proud new house. He made available to them the choicest timbers from his mills and dispatched his ships to South America to bring in rare decorative woods for special features.

There seems to be no record of whether Carson was aided by an architect in designing his house. If an architect was involved he was a man of fanciful imagination. Perhaps if the designer had been a man of conventional taste, a follower of the customary architectural styles of the period, the Carson Mansion would now be just another big house and William Carson scarcely remembered at all. But the house that was designed is one of the most extraordinary dwellings in the country. By a curious transposition of fame, William Carson himself is almost forgotten but the house he planned as a memorial to himself has become one of the most famous houses in the West, pictured in most books about California and photographed by thousands of motorists who travel the Redwood Highway, US 101, that passes in front of it.

All sorts of words have been used to describe William Carson's memorial mansion, not all of them flattering. They include grotesque, bizarre, fanciful, ridiculous, pretentious and one that everyone will agree to, unique. The house has eighteen spacious rooms and wide porches. From steep roofs rise a forest of gables and pinnacles capped by a high tower under a peaked pyramid roof. There are balconies framed with cast-iron railings, tucked into gables, filling every odd corner and extending on brackets from the top of the tower. Those who try to classify the style of the Carson Mansion have hit upon the term Victorian-Gothic. Certainly there are vague suggestions of the pointed Gothic arch, and enormous quantities of scroll-saw and wood-lathe work.

Carson wanted his remarkable house to be the finest there was. To that end he not only used redwood timbers wherever they could be employed but for interior details imported shiploads of rare primavera from South America. Primavera is a sleek and beautifully grained light-colored hardwood. It was used throughout the house for arched recesses, soaring

Bizarre and amazing, sometimes called a Victorian monstrosity, the mansion William Carson built at Eureka, California, as a memorial to himself is constructed almost entirely of redwood, a timber that made a fortune for the builder of the house. *Photograph: Courtesy Redwood Empire.*

staircases and lofty panels carved in intricate designs. And it was used as a frame for the most curious interior feature of the house, a carved fireplace of solid onyx from Mexico, designed with a remarkable double flue that permitted a window of stained glass, depicting a coy medieval maid, to be installed over the mantel.

When the house was finished in 1886 newspaper writers and others invited to see it called it the finest house in the West, some going so far as to describe it as the most splendid mansion in the country. It wasn't, of course, but it was certainly one of the strangest and most remarkable. Carson lived for twenty-six years after the house was completed, dwelling proudly in his ornate and fanciful home. When he died in 1912 his was the biggest funeral ever held in Eureka. His family continued to live in the mansion until 1950, when it was acquired by a private club, the Ingomar Club, which maintains it as a social center of Eureka and for the delight of visitors. The house is kept up in a manner that Carson would have approved, sparkling under fresh coats of spinach, cream and ebony paint that help achieve a climax of fantasy on wide porches that girdle the lower floor, with roofs supported by grotesquely bulbed scrollwork pillars.

Some who live in Eureka today still remember William Carson. They should. He built a house that has made their town famous throughout the West. Visitors find it easily, on the edge of Eureka, just off US 101, ironically forty miles south of the new Redwood National Park that is preserving thousands of the majestic trees that William Carson worked so hard to destroy.

Grotesquely bulbous pillars, painted spinach, cream, and black, support the porch roof of the mansion. *Photograph: Courtesy Redwood Empire.*

Odd interior detail of the Carson Mansion is a carved fireplace of solid onyx with a double flue, permitting a window of stained glass above the fireplace itself. *Photograph: Courtesy Redwood Empire.*

240

INDEX

Page numbers in italics *refer to illustrations.*